Copyright © Jade Chen, 2020 and 2022

All rights reserved. No part of this book may be reproduced in any form without permission in writing from the author. Reviewers may quote brief passages in reviews.

Published 2020 as e-book; revised and published as paperback in 2022.

DISCLAIMER

No part of this publication may be reproduced or transmitted in any form or by any means, mechanical or electronic, including photocopying or recording, or by any information storage and retrieval system, or transmitted by email without permission in writing from the author.

Neither the author nor the publisher assumes any responsibility for errors, omissions, or contrary interpretations of the subject matter herein. Any perceived slight of any individual or organization is purely unintentional.

Brand and product names are trademarks or registered trademarks of their respective owners.

*Dedicated to my son, Alaka'i,
and all who heed the call of Spirit ~*

Table of Contents

Chapter 1: Kāhea (The Call)

Chapter 2: The Radiant Lotus

Chapter 3: Phoenix Rising

Chapter 4: Pledge Allegiance to Your Soul & Its Purpose

Chapter 5: Harness Your Sacred Time & Space

Chapter 6: Own Your Own Authority

Chapter 7: Embrace Your Emotions

Chapter 8: Neutralize Your Mind

Chapter 9: Illuminate Your Speech

Chapter 10: X. Make Your Mark, Claim Your Crown & Master Your Domains

Chapter 11: When Heaven's Burning

Chapter 12: Love Prevails All Trauma

Acknowledgements

Thank You

P.S.
About The Author

Chapter 1:
Kāhea (The Call)

Aloha Dear One,

Thank you for heeding the call to read this. It takes a certain kind of person to pick up this book, and I honor your heart and soul that led you to do so.

This book is a love letter and treasure map that I am sending to you through the grid and across time and space to share with you some "mana" – some life force, and some encouragement as you rebuild your wings and rebirth yourself.

I invite you to take a moment and just breathe. If you can, feel free to close your eyes and just take some deep breaths. And if you like, please place one hand on your heart and one hand on your belly, as you take a few more deep inhales and exhales. It's time to come home and strengthen your core Soul Self.

I am speaking to you from the womb of the planet where the newest land on Earth gets born. I built a Temple here, at Pele's feet – the Hawaiian Goddess of Volcanoes and Transformation.

PeleHonuamea -- she who births and destroys in the same breath – she has allowed me to live here through three different volcanic eruptions near my home, raise my boy child here, and also to welcome other Soul Seekers to this Cauldron of Transformation. We call her "Tutu" – grandma. We know that those who are meant to hear the call will hear it and respond.

But decades ago, I was the one lying awake at night, wondering if this is all there is to life. Lying on the floor heartbroken or sleepwalking through the days as they faded into grey.

I know what it's like to feel trapped, helpless or uninspired in a relationship, wondering how to get to the place where Love lives.

I know what it's like to be working in a crazy, tedious or insane job, forty, sixty, eighty hours a week at times, just making the money and paying the bills, yet starved on a soul-level.

I know what it's like to be living in an artificial matrix urban world, blocking out all the noisy billboards, all the vying for our attention, all the stresses and strains of urban living. I remember stomping around those concrete city streets, desperate for a slice of sky between the buildings, feeling disconnected and cold.

I know what it's like to feel like you have to constantly navigate a tight minefield of other people's desires, expectations, triggers, and agendas. And wondering, *"Will I ever be free? When will I ever be free? How can I get free?"*

I know what it's like to feel like no matter what, you never measure up, that you're never enough, never good enough, never worthy. And wondering if you will ever feel truly happy or okay.

I spent much of my early life conforming, people-pleasing, and putting everyone else first. The result of a toxic cocktail of Catholic school, Christian martyrdom, traditional Asian parents, and being born female -- all that kind of early conditioning had me suppress and repress myself for decades, to contort into an empty, people-pleasing puppet shell of who I truly am. Not to mention a few years of physical and sexual abuse and over one hundred incidences of stranger assault growing up in ghetto NYC (before it was gentrified) -- all of which I just shrugged off and suppressed for many years.

Decades of fawning, hiding "the unsightly parts," pushing down traumas and contorting into what others wanted us to be, so we can avoid upsetting family and fit into society, and earn all the accolades and rewards of the external players in our orbit.

Then perhaps having all the signs of outward success but still feeling vaguely unhappy, like something's missing... Is this all there is? Is this life?

How much of ourselves have we locked away? How many traumas have we just buried somewhere deep? Swept under the rug? How many little girls and boys, frozen in time, have disassociated and hid or fled away?

Will we ever get them back? All those soul fragments... will we ever be whole? Happy? Free?

Maybe we try out therapy or this course or that reiki session and perhaps they do help us to an extent. And yet, there's that nagging sense of the old traumas, perhaps from childhood, or perhaps inherited from the family line, that we feel are still there, tightly locked away, subconsciously draining our energy or dooming us to repeat old limiting patterns. Maybe we feel compelled to sabotage our own successes, the possibilities of happiness and love, yet we are not quite sure why.

Perhaps we still wake up and do the thousand things and feed the kids and perform, and sometimes we feel a tinge of fleeting joy and occasionally we feel on top of the world -- and yet perhaps a lot of the time, we feel numb or worse.

Perhaps we've become very good at the "freeze, fight, flee, and fawn" -- the four major trauma responses and all the ways that we strategize to survive another day…

Yet, is there another way?

Dear One, it is dawn now, and I am here, at my Magical Lava Temple in an elemental paradise, writing this to you as a double rainbow stretches wide across the horizon ~ in the hopes of throwing you a lifeline back to who you truly are ~ your Primal Divinity. Your truest Soul Self, and the You that You are meant to be. Grace threw me one decades ago and it is only fitting that I extend one to you.

Thank you for picking up this book, Beloved One.
I believe in you.
Thank you for heeding the call.

* * *

Chapter 2:
The Radiant Lotus

WINTER.

"I'm done. I can't do this anymore." I remember chanting that over and over while lying on the floor in my family's NYC loft. I had collapsed there after a fight with my brother, and it was the fourth day in a row, of collapsing on the floor, shaking with stress, my nervous system shot. I couldn't work anymore. I couldn't do anything anymore. *"I'm done, God. Thank you, but I'm done."*

2006 had been a dark night of the Soul. I had lost everything.

The year prior, I had been on top of the world, managing a $5 million investment portfolio, building seven international art and real estate companies with my family in SoHo, and training as a Blackbelt in HapKiDo in the evenings. My nickname was "Killer" as I loved fierce full-contact fighting. I collected weapons and wore my bruises with pride. I met my then fiancé there at the dojang – a fellow jaguar warrior with dark eyes and a pure heart. We fell in love and decided to backpack around Central America together for a few months before I returned to graduate school.

We flew to Tucson, Arizona and then took every creaky chicken bus from the Mexican border to the heights of San Cristobal de las Casas and then across sketchy-ass border towns in Chiapas, to enter into breathtaking Guatemala. We prayed in Mayan pyramids in Quetzaltenango, explored the amber markets of Antigua and then rented an off-grid Spanish-style casita on the shores of Lago de Atitlan - a collapsed volcanic crater lake.

In the daytime, we would sing songs, play capoeira, or take the little boat to the nearby town Panajachel. I would check on my option trades in the internet café, and then we would enjoy fresh chamomile tea and treats, and then take the little boat back to San Pedro where the landlady would make us dinner. On our last week there, we hiked up to a sacred remote mountain lake and exchanged coconut shell rings and engagement vows, planning to marry in 2010.

Then 2006 hit.

"Be careful, Jade. Life comes in cycles, and you are entering your winter time, you need to be conservative and not take many risks. You need to rest. Keep what you have and save up your energy for when your Springtime comes back." My dear Aunt Alice, a master at Taiwanese Divination, had warned me prior.

I didn't listen. We had returned to Arizona where I was balancing risky options daytrading with writing my graduate thesis for my MFA in Poetry. The Fannie Mae scandal came out and the stock market – and my portfolio -- started crashing. So I woke up earlier and stayed up later and traded more, and ended up losing even more money. Some days I would "win" $50k; only to lose $100k the next. I started losing so much of my family's money that I literally felt my hair turn white and my adrenals turn cold, as I struggled to dig myself out of the debt pit that I had spiraled into when the market tanked. Glued to my three blinking laptops from 6am – 10pm, l neglected everything and everyone else. I barely finished my Masters' Thesis and my Beloved missed me. As I became a shell of my former self, he started looking elsewhere, and I lost him too.

After we broke up, I returned to NYC to try to rest and regroup in my family's home; but they weren't having it. They were all workaholics, building an art and real estate empire, and demanded that I work like usual. I could barely get out of bed. After the last fight where I lay spasming on the floor for four days, I finally dragged myself to a doctor.

"Oh my God, Jade. Your immune system is flatlined and in the negative. Your hypothyroidism is so severe that you could slip into a coma. Your adrenals are beyond shot. You seriously need to rest and detox. Have you ever heard of the Optimum Health Institute?"

I booked a ticket and spent three weeks there. Wheatgrass shots, colonics, raw food, juicing, toning, yoga – all these were new to me. I had always been an intense, urban martial artist – daytrader – warrior who powered through everything and shrugged off any hurts. I used to think *"yoga was boring and for wimps!"* Yet life had brought me to my knees, and I now surrendered to a softer way of being. After two weeks, I started feeling alive again. On the third week, I had a heart to heart with God:

"Ok, God. If I am to live, I vow to live it by Spirit. Forget everyone else, and all of their agendas and expectations. Forget society and family, and all of their constant wants and demands. I promise to listen to Spirit first and foremost. To cherish my heart and soul, and live life by their guidance. I am open to a new life, with Grace as my co-pilot..."

I quit my multiple jobs in NYC. I stopped training intense martial arts. I told my family I was on sabbatical. I flew back to Arizona and bought a red Toyota Tacoma with a camper shell, put a futon mattress in the back and installed spring green curtains, and it became my new home. Truckie Roja, I called her.

I lived out of my truck for three years as I became a spiritual nomad, going wherever Spirit called me. Solo and in silence, I spent weeks fasting and praying in different deserts and forests and mountaintops. All the busyness of my past life faded away and the still, small voice of my Soul got clearer and clearer. I lived mostly on water mixed with Vitamineral Green powder and shed thirty pounds. When I wasn't meditating, I was studying wellness, detoxing, shamanism, soul retrieval, plant medicine, energy medicine, etc.

In 2009, I landed in Los Angeles and spent nine months at a Kundalini Yoga Teacher Training, learning how to harness my Kundalini life force. I received the spiritual name "Rajbir Kaur" – "Princess of God who embodies Royal Courage." My spirit was shining again. I felt reborn.

* * *

SPRING.

Honoring my Spirit, daily Kundalini Yoga, and a healthy yogic lifestyle brought me back to vibrant health. By 2009, I felt magnificent! I was ready to root down and begin a new life.

So then the question was where. Sedona? NYC? Los Angeles?

I did an astrocartography reading with an expert named Julian Lee to find out where would be the best places on the planet for me.

Julian asked, *"Well Jade, what do you want? Money? Fame? Career? Success?"*

"I want my Spiritual Evolution," I stated.

Julian looked at my chart and after a few days, he called me and said, "*You need to go to the Big Island of Hawaii or Melbourne, Australia for the next twelve years or so."*

At first, I was put off.

"Hawaii? Isn't it super touristy?" I had only been there once for a whirlwind week with a German model I was dating, and we had done all the touristy things. I hadn't been impressed. But I

decided to buy a ticket and check it out. I found a little Balinese hut on the coastline of Puna for $400 and I booked it for a month.

I landed in Hilo airport on October 20th, 2009. As soon as I got off the plane, there was something about the quality of the light and the air, and I immediately felt that I was on sacred ground. The urge -- *"I must build a temple here"* – came to me over and over. The desire increased all month as life flowed very magically. I woke up to rainbows and fresh papayas, dancing butterflies, and dolphins jumping out of the ocean. I would hike in the jungle and admire the love stories of the trees as they weaved canopies of light and shadow. I felt the vibrant souls of the plants as they offered their medicine. In short, it was heaven.

I started teaching Kundalini Yoga every day as a free service to the community. Neighbors would arrive knocking at my door at 8 am, and I would go upstairs and teach whomever showed up. I started hosting New Moon Dream Circles and Full Moon Healing Rings of White Tantra. People offered papayas, avocados and flowers as payment.

And then the month passed, and I was supposed to fly back to New York City for the holidays. But something urged me to stay and at the last minute, I didn't get on the plane. Instead, I stayed another month, teaching yoga, hosting more events, and listening into the magic. My friend Stephen flew in to do a photoshoot of me along the majestic Puna coastline. On the way, I picked up a hitchhiker. His name was William. We started talking and ended up spending the whole day together as Stephen photographed us all along the coast.

William was one of the most interesting people I'd ever met. He had lived in Tiger caves in Nepal doing his solo three-year retreat and became one of the first Westerners to become a Tibetan Buddhist Lama. Decades later, he was tucked away in the Hawaiian rain forest, hitchhiking a ride with me.

As he shared some of his life story with me, I told him, *"Wow, you've been through a lot! So have I. The only thing I haven't done yet is I haven't become a Mother -- but I would only do that if I could raise a Buddha."*

The world stopped. He looked at me piercingly and whispered slowly, *"Me too."* And then, just like that, it was like we were under a spell. Spirit heard us and imprinted a divine date with destiny.

I spent my last day in Hawaii on the Malama Ki flats, alone and communing with the ocean. A mother and baby whale appeared in front of me, and stayed for hours, as I counted 108 blows before they swam off. What a beautiful way to say *"a hui ho" – "goodbye for now."*

I flew back to NYC, and William and I became best friends over the phone. I would work all day in my family's SoHo Art Gallery, teach Kundalini Yoga in the evenings, and then I would call William in Hawaii and talk to him till the wee hours of the morning. After a few months, I decided to return to the Big Island to participate in some Ayahuasca Ceremonies and to explore what Spirit wanted to have unfold.

Around Springtime, I flew back and stayed a week at William's house, a large, open-air barn-like structure in the heart of the rainforest. He called it "The Palace of the Sky Bird," as 'ios (Hawaiian hawks) and pueos (Hawaiian short-eared owls) nested in the thick mango trees nearby and circled it, singing day and night. William was unlike any other man I had dated, but it felt like we were so spiritually aligned that it happened naturally that we made love.

The next day, I attended the medicine ceremony and a prayer came rising strong out of me that I had never prayed before, resounding and spiraling like a clear bell up and up into the heavens -- *"If I cannot liberate all sentient beings, then may I give birth to one who can!"*

Over and over and over, that prayer spiraled within me and up into the heavens, for several hours. The ceremony ended and I flew to Shanghai the next day to help my parents at my father's Art Exhibition at the World Expo.

On the plane ride, I had a dream. I was in the great ocean of all consciousness. I saw and felt William's lineage and his stream of consciousness, all of his ancestral thread. I saw and felt the stream of consciousness of my own family's lineage and origins. And then there was a third stream that came surfing and dancing in, between us, and it was bursting with so much joy.

I arrived in Shanghai, looked in the mirror and felt instinctively like my body was different. I called William up in Hawaii and I told him about the dream and about my body, and he said, *"Jade, that's our child."* I was shocked. We had only made love once. I had him write a letter to introduce himself to my family. And then instead of helping my family with the 2010 Shanghai World Expo, I ended up temple shopping for items to decorate our home. With suitcases full of Tara statues, thangkas, altar cloths, silk brocade, jade daggers, metal phurbas and such, I flew back to Hawaii in June to start our pregnancy journey together. We transformed the Palace of the Sky Bird into the Temple of Green Tara, as we awaited the birth of our son.

*   *   *

SUMMER.

In our Temple of Green Tara, I would wake up every morning in the amrit vela hours (before dawn) and do my Kundalini Yoga sadhana (spiritual practice). It generally consisted of a cold shower, chanting the JapJi (Sihk prayers), and also doing a certain meditation called Kirtan Kriya. Kirtan Kriya is considered one of the highest kriyas for women, it balances and integrates all the cycles of life, as well as clears out psychic imprints from past partners. My intention was to clear my auric field completely and make sure that I did not pass down any negative karma to our child. I ended up practicing 1,000 days of it to gain the benefits of mastering the meditation. William and I both believed our role as parents was to primarily help our child fulfill his spiritual destiny. Spirit had chosen us to be spiritual partners in this endeavor (not to be traditional parents or romantic partners).

As William and I awaited our child, we often swam in the Mermaid Ponds nearby and read books. One of the book series that we were deeply inspired by was Anastasia's *"Ringing Cedars Series,"* which talks about having a *"Space of Love"* – an approximately two acre plot of land with a food forest where a child would ideally be conceived, birthed, and grow up in harmony with nature. The food from that land would be the best medicine possible and keep the child healthy and strong for their entire life. We dreamed of creating that in Hawai'i and since we couldn't buy the land that we were on, we spent our days looking for another piece of land to create our homestead–Temple – our *"space of love."*

Kundalini Yoga has a body of wisdom within it, pertaining to Conscious Conception, Pregnancy, Birth, and the first few years of life. I studied it in detail and enacted many of the meditations and practices to ensure the best possible environment for our child to be born in. On the 120th day, we celebrated the Soul coming into the body and hosted a beautiful "Blessingway" at our Temple home.

And then it was time. I went into labor, and our two midwives and doula came to our side. Twenty-four hours passed and I was only dilated 4cm. Night came and William lit a bonfire. At one point, the midwives started getting worried and talked of taking me to the hospital, which was more than an hour away from the remote jungle temple we were in.

But then, I felt something shift – I raised my right hand and exclaimed, *"Wait!"* and within ten minutes gave birth right there on the carpet.

Alaka'i Ulimana Braham was born twenty minutes after Mercury went direct on December 29th, 2010 in the evening time, at the Temple of Green Tara, in Kapoho, Puna District of the Big Island of Hawai'i. We immediately had him skin-to-skin and nursing. We did a lotus birth, which consisted of keeping his umbilical cord connected to his placenta until it naturally fell off. The placenta had been like his brother in the womb all this time and held precious vital nutrients for him. Hospitals often don't realize how important the placenta is and they clamp the bloodflow and cut the cord too soon. We allowed Alaka'i to be connected to his placenta for three days, carting it around in a metal bowl with ice. We then seasoned the placenta with herbs, dried it in the sun, and cooked some of it for me to eat (helps restore vital nutrients to the mother after giving birth), and saved half of it to bury under a bodhi tree as Alakai's birth tree.

We also instituted the "Forty Day Blessing." For forty days, me and baby stayed at home and limited visitors, allowing for the baby to enjoy a gentle, peaceful welcome to the world. A baby's nervous system is just developing, they have no barriers or defenses yet and so they just absorb the vibratory frequencies all around them. So it's important to not overstimulate or traumatize them as they are so new and just forming. On the fortieth day, we took Alaka'i out into the world and naturally baptized him in the fresh ocean water. It was a sweet, special time.

*   *   *

AUTUMN.

William and I searched and searched for the right piece of land to create our homestead, our *"Space of Love"* and we just couldn't find the right spot. But then one day, I woke up and felt this strong calling to go to the bottom of Puna, past the end of the road, and into the lava fields at the foot of the Volcano. We had never yet gone out to the old lava flows. I felt this urgent need and the next day we drove out to Kalapana.

As soon as the black lava landscape rolled out in front of me, and I saw the slope of the volcano ahead, I fell in love. This was absolutely my spirit environment. We rolled up and immediately on the left, there was a "For Sale Sign" on a house. The next door neighbor saw us checking it out and waved and said, *"the house is open if you want to go inside and take a look!"* We walked in and went upstairs, it was just a rustic shell of a house, but I was enthralled. From the window, one could see the Kilauea shield volcano and a smoky cloud atop that signaled Halema'uma'u crater where Tutu Pelehonuamea lived – Goddess of Volcanos and Transformation. I felt my heart leap with joy and awe.

"William, I know that this is it!"

He looked at me quizzically and said, *"Why would you want to live here, Jade? This place is like a charnel ground. Why would you want to raise a family here?"*

I prayed silently, *"Okay, Spirit, if this is the place, please give me a sign. You have to give me a sign."*

And a rainbow literally materialized right then in the cloudless sky.

I jumped and said, *"William, look! I asked for a sign and that rainbow appeared."*

He studied me a bit, and then said, *"Okay, Jade, if you really feel so strongly about it, I would be willing to live here and make a life with you here."*

As soon as he said that, it became a double rainbow. I bought the house in November 2011, and we woke up to double rainbows every day stretching across the vast expanse of space and sky for months. We started to make our life out on the barren lava and fill in this shell of a house. We added solar panels, batteries, an inverter and generator for power. We added gutters and a catchment system to catch the rainwater. William started making lava rock walls with his bare hands and planting fragrant flowers and coconut palms. It was wonderful to be able to make a nest and spend our first Christmas as a family with baby Alaka'i on the lava at Pele's feet.

Soon after, I designed and built the Lava Temple a few steps away – it was an off-grid, two-level, open-air Temple space, bathed in reds and golds. At first, it was a place to teach yoga; but then I started cozying it up and running it as an Airbnb.

Over the years, the Magical Lava Temple became a place of refuge, celebration, and healing for so many. Family reunions, traditional Hawaiian weddings, healing immersions, kundalini yoga retreats, rebirthing workshops, sound baths, soul clearings, medicine ceremonies – the list goes on. I hosted thousands upon thousands of amazing guests from all around the world to come and enjoy this elemental vortex – and reconnect with their own primal Self as well.

One summer, I was helping out at Mehtab Benton's Kundalini Yoga and Sound Healing Immersion at Kalani (the local retreat center) nearby. I met a gorgeous young man there named Will Beilharz, and he spent his birthday at the Lava Temple. A pueo flew in and kept him company that night as he communed with Pele in that elemental vortex. Turns out he was an architect and Founder of Artistree Homes, and the next day he told me he was interested in building an off-grid tiny home near me and having me manage it. Thus, birthed the ubercool Phoenix House which has now been acclaimed in media worldwide and is one of the most amazing tiny homes in the world.

A few years later, I hosted a sweet family from Virginia and led them through family yoga. We all enjoyed a lovely time, and they were also enchanted by the raw elemental power of the place. The very next day, Sam and Erica bought two lots right behind me, and hired Will to build a "tiny home for families." Thus was born the Ohana House, and my Magical Lava Sanctuary grew. Since then, we have expanded even more and often host groups of up to sixteen, for meditation / yoga / healing retreats and vacations.

For several years, Pele the Smoking Goddess let down her sensual molten rivers of lava locks right in front of us. We watched in awe and reverence as her fiery-gold rivers weaved down the slopes and into the ocean, causing a huge smoke plume, and forming the newest land on earth. At night, the sky would glow red, and you could almost feel Pele dancing in her crater home nearby. Day and night, smoke and steam rose from her folds, and a steady stream of pilgrims hiked through to witness this magnificent dance of destruction and creation.

Even though we were only four miles away from the feet of the world's most active volcano, I never felt scared or threatened by the lava. I always felt blessed and nurtured by God – Grace – Spirit – Divine Mother – whatever you want to call it – and blessed to be the *"Konohiki"* (chosen caretaker of sacred land). I felt like Pele had called me to her side and had given me a safe space to heal and reconnect with my divine true nature. A refuge for the mud to settle and my Lotus Heart to open and blossom again. A sanctuary for my Soul's Rebirthing. And to provide this gift for others as well.

The secret name for my Lava Sanctuary is the Adi Shakti Refuge. Adi Shakti means *"The Primal Female Force of All Creation"* – of which Pele is an embodiment of this Divine Creatrix Energy as she births the newest land on earth nearby. This place is a *"Cauldron of Transformation"* as well as a *"Cup of Prayer."* Darkness transmutes quickly here, dreams manifest and prayers get answered at lightning speed. The sun beats strong, the wind often shakes the house, the rain rushes to cleanse, and the black lava ionic earth absorbs all negativity. And the sweeping views of sky and stars take one's breath away. Wild hawks, owls, and pheasants have flown into the Temple and kept us company. A perfect place in majestic nature to sit and get clear, to birth new books, projects, or just one's next golden chapter of one's life.

So besides the adventurous tourists, I hosted many who felt called to come for Private Healing Retreats. Before Hawaii, I had been a Life Coach, Martial Arts Teacher, and "self-development junkie." I had spent my teens and twenties studying different modalities in the arenas of leadership, performance, success, communication, transformation, possibility, and such – mostly with Landmark Education and Tony Robbins' Mastery University and Leadership Academy. In the past two decades, I came to fuse those skillsets with the ancient yogic bodies of wisdom regarding Kundalini life force, White Tantra, Shadow

Alchemy, Energy Work and the multidimensional self – as well as Plant Medicines, Ancestral Healing and Akashic Record Reading. I also trained to become a Family Constellations Facilitator and enjoy drawing from that body of wisdom to help heal generational wounds and bring clients' family / business dynamics into their proper order.

Over the years, my gifts as a Spiritual Guide and Healer became stronger and deeper, and I became better and better at uncovering and healing old wounds, clearing trauma out of the body and helping unleash the natural life force that my clients had blocked or frozen away. Together, we would also uncover the old, limiting beliefs that they had made to survive, that kept them limited and self-sabotaging; and make new Vows in service to their highest good. It was such fulfilling work to see my clients enjoy more clarity, freedom, peace, power and happiness in their lives. Many come back every year, and receive Soul Clearings for themselves and their family members.

In 2012, I founded a company called **The Radiant Lotus**. For me, the lotus is a supreme symbol of purity. No matter what vile filth or dark mud surrounds this flower, it would still rise up and blossom beautifully and radiant. I saw this as a symbol of our own true nature – that no matter what pain, hardship or injustice had happened in our own lives, that our essential nature is always still whole, complete, pure, and inviolable. And that when we can dwell in that certainty, we can live life with grace and ease, as well as great love and compassion for ourselves and others. When we can remember and live from our own innate divine nature, the other mundane drama-trauma crap of the external world doesn't need to affect us so much. We learn ways to alchemize the pain into power. We can transmute trauma into treasure. We can weave wounds into wisdom. We can build temples of love amidst the chaos.

I also believe that our Souls can choose which conditions to incarnate into, and that some of the bravest of us have chosen to incarnate into deep darkness. All the more so that we can shine brighter and triumphant once we remember who we truly are and why we are here. So, we learn that perhaps everything that has happened in life, happened FOR us, not TO us, and that any darkness just allows us to shine even brighter, to create more contrast to allow for more and greater redemption and victory.

In Hawaiian mythology, they talk of each of us coming into the world with a *"bowl of light"* – a gift from our *'aumakua* – our ancestors. As time goes on, rocks start to come into our bowl of light, whenever we injure or are injured by others. Our light dims, and life can feel difficult and even unbearable at times. Yet I see these rocks as like geodes -- which when cracked open with loving awareness – will release light, treasure and lifeforce. I believe these wounds are where our power is oftentimes hidden.

So it's my honor to provide a safe space where we can lean into these hard places; and shine the conscious light of awareness into the pain we have hidden away. I help people to alchemize their darkness, to clear trauma out of their body, to release addictions, to clear lifetimes of grief and shame, all this so that we may free up the frozen energy – which I refer to as the Kundalini lifeforce. The Hawaiians have a term for it also – *"mana"* – which is a spiritual energy and healing power that pervades the universe, people and certain locations. Once we transmute the darkness and free up that lifeforce again, we can then utilize that restored energy in service to your health and happiness. As we reclaim our lifeforce, as we remember our Divine Identity and Purpose, we can rise above all adversity and chaos to create the Soul-Centered, Ideal Life that truly fulfills us and brings us joy.

Helping people to do this – personally, financially and generationally – has become my life's work now. I am honored to hold the Divine Mother Frequency of Unconditional Love and to empower you in transforming your trauma into treasure and freeing you up towards your brilliant, resilient, liberated life.

*   *   *

Chapter 3:
Phoenix Rising –

"Once you start to awaken, no one can ever claim you again for the old patterns.

Now you realize how precious your time here is. You are no longer willing to squander your essence on undertakings that do not nourish your true self; your patience grows thin with tired talk and dead language. You see through the rosters of expectation which promise you safety and the confirmation of your outer identity.

Now you are impatient for growth, willing to put yourself in the way of change. You want your work to become an expression of your gift. You want your relationship to voyage beyond the pallid frontiers to where the danger of transformation dwells. You want your God to be wild and to call you to where your destiny awaits."

– John O' Donohue

Dear One, I share with you some of these stories to hopefully inspire you to commit to your own healing journey, transmute your own darkness and create your own ideal life. While I was living it, I never knew how it would all unfold. Listening to Spirit is often like following a trail of faint breadcrumbs. We just have to be watchful for signs, keep the faith, and keep showing up.

I've learned a lot of things the hard way. My whole life, I had wished for teachers, gurus, coaches who could help show me the way and quicken my learning curve. Though I don't have any set guru I am connected with, I learned to bow down and make Life itself my teacher, everyone and every experience my teacher.

In my obsession with self-growth and transformation, I have immersed myself in mastering many modalities that can assist in empowering us to live at our fullest potential. In writing this book, I've compiled some best practices so that I can pass this on to as many as I can, to assist in the tipping point of consciousness towards an enlightened society. I know that when enough of us have risen up and beyond our traumas, reclaimed our life force and destiny, and are contributing our gifts to society, then this world will be a heaven on earth.

So I leave you this treasure map to help you rebirth your Soul Self. To navigate out of darkness and rise up from the ashes, toward the fuller, wiser, happier version of the highest You. You can dwell wherever you need to on this journey. You don't have to do it in order. And please don't take any of it as *"The Absolute*

Truth." We are all such different, multidimensional Beings, and different tools and methodologies will work with different people and at different times in our lives. There is no "one way" up the mountain. Please, just try on these tools, keep what fits, and discard what doesn't. Just absorb what you can as lessons will often spiral back upon each other.

A symbol that is deeply meaningful to me in many ways is the Phoenix. In Asian mythology, the phoenix is a radiant creature that arises from the ashes of death to be reborn. As someone who has experienced quite a few dark nights of the soul in my lifetime, I would hold fast to the image of the fiery phoenix as I rebirthed myself back into life. Each of us is constantly dying and being born again in many ways, so perhaps you can relate. Thus, I leave you with the Phoenix Process.

The Phoenix Process:

A Treasure Map to Rebirth Your Soul Self.
To guide your healing journey as you release past trauma, own your Primal Divinity, and propel you forward into your Ideal, Soul-Aligned Life.

P: Pledge Allegiance to Your Soul & Its Purpose
(Make the Commitment & Set the Intentions)

H: Harness Your Sacred Time & Space
(Lay down the Foundation for the Journey to unfold)

O: Own Your Own Authority
(Anchor into Your Own Sovereignty & Self-Worth)

E: Embrace Your Emotions
(Mastering Emotions and Honoring those Messengers)

N: Neutralize Your Mind
(Aligning with Infinite Wisdom)

I: Illuminate your Speech
(Cultivating Conscious Communication)

X: Make Your Mark, Claim Your Crown and Master Your Domains
(Embody Your Royal Divinity & Create Your Ideal Life)

(* In my Masterminds, there is a season of support, with live coaching calls, access to a Wisdom Video Library, 1:1 Soul Clearings and Constellations, more in-depth meditations and exercises, as well as the option of in-person Retreats to support the integration of your transformation over time. In this e-book format, I am limited in what I can include as supplementary resources, but I will include what I can in "Recommendations" that follow each chapter. They are purely optional, of course.)

Kundalini Yoga

I have found some of the best tools for embodying one's Divine True Nature lie within the ancient wisdom of Kundalini Yoga. It is a *"Raj Yog,"* a royal form of yoga that was previously only taught to the royal caste in India. In the 1960's, one of my teachers, Yogi Bhajan, brought it to the Western World. This royal form of yoga encompasses many different tools and techniques, all designed to free up and harness your Kundalini life-force, your *"mana,"* to enlighten your consciousness and enrich your life. It is a science of awakening that uses sound, mantra, energy healing, exercises and meditations to release trauma from the energetic body, which surrounds the physical body. It is this field, known as the aura, that holds wounds. When those wounds are healed, radiance can occur. Mantras are like exalted frequencies that can evoke a certain kind of effect. For example, some mantras evoke protection or wealth or healing or victory, etcetera. Another tool we use is called a *"kriya,"* which basically means a completed action, technique or practice meant to achieve a specific result.

In this book, I will share some relevant mantras and kriyas that can help to anchor in the message of the theme.

Recommendations:

1). If you don't have these yet – please get a Journal and create a little Altar and Meditation area for yourself. It doesn't have to be anything fancy, I have been writing in plain, college-ruled spiral notebooks for decades, and I have several little tables around my house that serve as Altars, as well as a meditation cushion and yoga mat nearby. Just carve out a cozy little area for yourself and have some tools that are purely for your Soul's nourishment. Please use this Journal to write down your Intentions for this journey, as well as any insights, notes, etc.

Ok, I look forward to deep diving together! ~

Chapter 4:
Pledge Allegiance to Your Soul & Its Purpose

"It is only by a change of consciousness that the true basis of life can be discovered: from within outward. But within does not mean some quarter inch behind the surface. One must go deep and find the soul, the (true) Self [behind the masks of the conditioned personality], the Divine Reality within us and only then can life become a true expression of what we can be instead of a blind and always repeated confused blur of the inadequate and imperfect thing we were.

The choice is between remaining in the old jumble and groping about in the hope of stumbling on some discovery or standing back and seeing the Light within till we discover and can build the Godhead within and without us."

– Sri Aurobindo

You probably already know that you are more than a meatsuit in a machine, more than a body, ego, identity, and all the roles that you play. You are more than your past and all that has happened to you.

It's time now though to bring who you truly are to the forefront and anchor in your Sovereign Soul Self! All that past conditioning was to bring you to this point where you can now pivot and move forward to create the Soul-Centered Life that you were really born to live.

It begins with remembering and embodying your true Identity, on a Soul Level, and operating from that paradigm on a daily basis.

Seeing yourself as a spark of divinity, incarnated into this world, given a human body, conditioned through circumstances, to enable you to now contribute in a specific way and help others cross the particular bridges that you have.

What if your Soul and its Purpose was your first and foremost reason for being?

What if you lived life from that premise?

What if you stopped all the crazy busyness to fulfill society and everyone else's demands of you?

What if you unsubscribed from everyone else's agendas and external measures of success?

What if instead you tuned in deeply to your Soul, the deepest part of you, and lived life with Spirit as your co-pilot?

What if everything that has ever happened to you in this life was for the purpose of your Soul's Evolution and expansion of awareness, and that now – if you wanted -- you can choose differently?

So to begin this journey, I invite you to commit to your Soul's Evolution. I invite you to pledge allegiance to and prioritize your Soul's unique purpose. I invite you to allow your Soul's voice to be your inner compass and guiding system as to what is really relevant and what is not. Allow your Soul Self to be the nucleus of your life. So that you may live with purpose and peace, and sidestep a lot of unnecessary drama-trauma and wasting of precious time, energy and life-force.

Over the course of this journey, I will be sharing tools and exercises to help you sensitize to your subtler aspects, and cultivate your multidimensional, divine self.

For now, just imagine that at one point, you were One with the One. You were Divinity Itself. And then you chose to play the "manifesting into form game," and after 16 billion incarnations, you finally arrived to this particular body, space and time, for a specific Soul purpose. And everything from the past was to inform you and prepare you as to what that is.

So feel into:

Who are you at your core essence?
What do you feel naturally drawn towards?
What lights you up?
What obstacles have you overcome?
What do you stand for?

If you could leave this world a better place, what legacy would you want to leave to it?

(And if you don't know the answers to these yet, I invite you to take some time and focus to inquire into these deeper questions of your existence.)

Once you answer these questions, you can begin to anchor yourself so deeply in your Soul path and purpose that nothing can throw you off of your blessed trajectory.

Recommended:

Mantras:

I want to share with you two of the most fundamental mantras in Kundalini Yoga. They are used to tune in to one's higher self, open up sacred space and begin one's practice.

The Adi Mantra is:
ONG NAMO GURU DEV NAMO:

"I bow to the subtle infinite wisdom that's always within me"

And

SAT NAM:

"Truth is my Identity."

When saying this mantra, we are identifying ourselves as Truth and we are bowing to the truth within us.

When saying it to each other as a greeting, it is similar to *"Namaste,"* and we are acknowledging each other as Truth.

If you can relate to yourself more as Truth and let that be your identity rather than any kind of egoic conditioning or role that you got put into, then your life can change. When you can relate to yourself and others on a soul level and see yourself and others as an embodiment of the force of Truth, then your relationships and existence on Earth take on a deeper kind of meaning.

We are not just meat suits in a machine, stuck in 3D reality and obliged to please and fulfill everyone else's wants and expectations of us. No, we can serve something higher; we can be guided by our Soul's Light and Truth.

Somatic Exercise:

Here is a basic somatic exercise that is my usual "go-to" in the morning, and whenever I want to get centered and back into my body. It can take less than one minute. You are invited to use it on a daily basis, as well as whenever needed.

With these exercises, we start tuning in more and more into our own field of awareness and using the physical body as the modulator. We sensitive ourselves to ourselves, becoming the Cause and Source of our own life, rather than default reacting to the external world around us.

Body Scan:

Sit quietly, taking long deep breaths.

If you like, place your hands on your heart and/or your belly.

Allow yourself to feel all that you feel.

Let it all arise.

Start to slowly scan your body with your own awareness, from like 6 inches above your head, and then slowly all the way down your head, your body, your legs, to your toes.

Feel what you feel.
Feel all that you feel, purely as "sensations."

Feel into where there may be some achiness or hurt, or stuck or blocked energy.

Golden Breath:

As you inhale, visualize gathering up Golden Life-force and Mana from the heavens;

As you exhale, visualize it cascading down upon you like a waterfall, washing over and through you, filling every gap and cell of your Being with gold lifeforce.

Continue to do this as long as you like.

This trains yourself to be the source of your own blessings, soother of your own hurts, and to more consciously cultivate your own lifeforce.

Chapter 5: Harness Your Sacred Time & Space

"Vibrate the Cosmos, and the Cosmos will clear your path"
- Yogi Bhajan

So Dear One, now that you've committed to your Soul's Evolutionary journey and committed to yourself as Truth, for this journey to be successful, you will need to carve out some time and space for it to unfold. Just like any other relationship, to cultivate a stronger, closer relationship with your Soul, you will need to set aside "quality time" to spend with it, or else nothing will change.

Even if it's only a few minutes a day, just create and carve out safe sacred space for yourself. Don't distract or numb out, really sit with yourself.

Remember that before Jesus started his active ministry, he first spent forty days in the wilderness communing with God. Moses also spent some days up on the mountaintop before he could come down and be a leader for his people.

We all need an incubation period, a safe, sacred container of time and space with a focused intention where we can tune the rest of the world out and tune into the relationship we are cultivating.

Mystics, saints, and sages all started out with a sacred period of time where they left all of society and the world and went alone into solitary silence, allowing the mud of the mind and all the voices of the world to settle down and tune out so that they could tune in to the quiet whisperings of their own soul nature. So that they could go deeply within and commune with Source.

In our modern days, we are constantly bombarded by technology. Everyone is vying for our attention as a currency. It's important to actively tune out the other distractions, so that you can tune into what's authentically best for you.

So be the Gatekeeper of your own Body, Mind and Spirit. Be the Good Steward of your Time, Space and Lifeforce. Stop giving it all away to others and feed it to yourself. Turn off your TVs and the news. Limit your social media scrolling. Avoid other people's drama or gossip. Cut down on anything and anyone that drains your energy. Only allow nourishing, uplifting energy into your field. Create a sadhana (daily spiritual practice) that works for you and your lifestyle, so that you can tune into your own Soul Self.

One of my favorite things in the world is to go on retreat. I love tuning out the external, mundane world and tuning into my own Soul and bettering myself in some way. Whether it's one day, or ten days, or whatever, there is so much power available in this deep diving into a safe container for a specific amount of time with a focused intent. I've seen miracles happen in just a weekend even, when it's created intentionally as a private retreat. So set aside a "sacred pause" to let the mud settle and commune with your own Soul Self. Otherwise it's just too easy to float on the surface of things and allow the external world and others to distract us, drain our lifeforce, and dictate our existence.

Here in Hawaii, I feel like I am in constant private retreat and communion with Source. As I run around my Magical Lava Sanctuary, I am constantly in view of the smoking volcano in the distance, the black lava fields glistening in the sun, the open expanse of sky and space, the shimmering rainbows, the dynamic wind, the quality of light and air. I am in dialogue with all the raw elements and devas of this land, and I am being nourished on a Soul level. And when I'm not on my own private retreat on my land, I am hosting customized retreats for others. Part of my life's mission is to hold that sacred transformative space, to host deep Healing Immersions, and customized retreats so that people can tune out of the surface mundane world and tune in to their own Source, their radiant Souls, and make quantum leaps forward into their true happiness and purpose.

So create your own sacred pauses, your own private moments of time and space for yourself on the daily, weekly, monthly, and yearly. Mark out your cosmic calendar, taking note of New Moons, Full Moons, Equinoxes and Solstices; and see if you can do something special for yourself on those potent portals of time. I generally plan on launching my major programs and teachings on those days. It's good to harness the amplified energy flowing in on those special currents of time.

Kundalini Yoga is an exceptional yoga in this day and age, as it is a householders' yoga. Not many of us can afford to just join a monastery or leave all worldly obligations to do a Three-Year Retreat. And so Kundalini Yoga is full of tools for the lay people who are busy with family, career, children, responsibilities, as well as urban householders that still want to tune in with Source, live a mystical life and feed the soul.

I encourage you to create a Sadhana (a daily spiritual practice) that feels beneficial and is workable for you. So that more and more it becomes something easy and effortless that you can integrate into your life to enhance your life. Even if you can just set aside a few minutes a day to just sit with yourself, feel what you feel, sit up and tune in, invite the unseen guides and guardians to support you in your life, and set your frequency for who you are that day. I usually do this when I wake up, and also before I teach, before an important meeting, before any difficult conversations, etc. It only takes about a minute or two to open up sacred space and set my frequency, so that regardless of what is happening around me, I know the truth of who I am and what my intended outcome is.

So just take small holy moments for yourself in the day to recenter yourself, connect with your Source, and remember your Primal Divinity – remember that you are Truth, you are Soul, you are Spirit incarnate.

Recommended:

Kundalini Yoga, Tune In

To open up sacred space or begin one's spiritual practice, we tune in to our Higher Self. Instructions are here:

http://theradiantlotus.org/kundalini-yoga-tune-in/

More info on Tuning In & Mantras here:
https://www.3ho.org/kundalini-yoga/mantra/kundalini-yoga-mantras

---

Be the Master and Good Steward of Your Time and Space

1). Acknowledge all the ways that you might be wasting precious time, energy and lifeforce in non-constructive or draining pursuits, and set limits and reduce them.

2). Embrace Calendar tools and other technology, to create structures that support the optimal management of your time, space, and energy.

Take your Calendar Year, and mark out all the New Moons, Full Moons, Fall and Spring Equinoxes, Winter and Summer Solstices.

Allow these potent days to be significant touchstones as you spend your time on Earth.

3). Mark out a sacred pause for yourself, within every day, within every week, within every month (perhaps on every New and Full Moon), and even perhaps a set sabbatical of healing and rest for you sometime during the year. Research events and gatherings in your area that celebrate these potent days and see if you can attend some.

Expanding Your Self-Care:

4).   Schedule in Weekly Self-Care of some kind, preferably something physical (Massage, Acupuncture, Craniosacral, etc.).

Begin to treat yourself like an honored guest, a Sovereign Queen/King, a Master, and a small child -- with devotion, gentleness, presence, and great care. When you make sure to prioritize your self-care, then you won't need to look outside yourself to others to meet your needs as much. You will also be able to care for others better because your cup will be more full.

Tuning into Your Home Space and Location:

5).   Feel into your home situation, does it feel safe and cozy for you? Conducive to your healing and growth? Do you have an area carved out for your altar and meditation practice (can be modest)? If not, please look into how you can transform your space so that it's more nurturing for you and your Soul Self.

6).   Extra: Tune into your geographic location to see if you're in the best place for your thriving, and also where are the other best places on Earth for you to travel, visit, live, work during your lifetime. (If you are not sure, I recommend doing an Astrocartography reading.)

Chapter 6:
Own Your Own Authority

"Vincit qui se vincit"
Conquer Yourself to Conquer All

Okay Dear, now that you've committed to your Soul's Evolution, and you've set aside the sacred time and space to cultivate your Soul Self and purpose, you now have the foundation to go further and deeper. And before you can master your external environment, you need to master your inner and internal environment.

My motto growing up used to be: "*Know yourself, and then be thyself and to thine own self be true.*" It's time now to really tune in with and get to know who you are, at your essential and deepest level, and embody that more and more.

So tuning into who you are beyond the meatsuit in a machine, beyond your thoughts, emotions, whims, past; beyond the name and the roles that society and your family gave you that you got conditioned with. And owning and embodying yourself as the Multidimensional Divine Being that you are -- Spirit Incarnate in this body temple for a breath of time and with a unique purpose.

Once you know yourself as this Divine Being, then it's time to own your own authority -- I invite you to decide that YOU are the ONE, the ultimate authority of your own life.

I invite you to commit to yourself as the Owner, the Author, the Hero, and the Master of your life.

I invite you to relate to yourself as the Primary Solution, the Change Agent, the Cause in the matter.

I invite you to see yourself as the Ultimate Gatekeeper to your Body, Mind, Heart & Spirit.

I invite you to embrace yourself as Good Enough, Worthy Enough, just ENOUGH -- and having everything you need within you – and dropping any other stories that say otherwise.

Take a moment, and place your hands on your body, and breathe all that in…

And now it's time to tap into all of the vast treasure that you have within you -- relating to yourself as a Treasure, a Gem, a Diamond with a thousand facets. And you can distance yourself from all that "surface self" and not overly identify with all that other stuff anymore. So you don't need to get run by your thoughts, taken over by your emotions, or identify with your past, anymore. This is actually a very liberating thing!

As you distance yourself from that shallower self, you can allow yourself to look at the culmination of your Beingness, and examine with curiosity and compassion, where the blocks are in your life force flow.

And instead of playing the Victim – Blame Game; and getting pummeled and stuck in the Victim – Perpetrator – Rescuer Triangle Dysfunction; you can just get beyond that whole disempowering dynamic. I know it can be hard, I used to sink into the Victim – Martyr- Savior pattern so much in my life and it took decades to de-condition that out of me. I would often "overgive" and rescue, and then get resentful and self-righteous when it wasn't returned (and of course it could never be fully returned). I would jump in and save people because I couldn't stand to see people fall or fail or suffer, and I would end up enabling their negative behavior and resenting them later for not being thankful enough. Any of this sound familiar?

I used to be compelled to be the Extraordinary Caregiver and Rescuer, and not know why; and then later learned that we often adopt that role as a survival mechanism. We learn to become indispensable so that no one in their right mind would leave us, so the tribe won't abandon us, so that we can belong in the world.

There are all kinds of unconscious and subconscious programs and vows that will keep on running and compelling us, until we shine the light of conscious awareness on them and rework a new vow, a new program that empowers us. These defense mechanisms are not bad or wrong, it's just that we want to be able to choose when to use them, when they are appropriate and in the highest good, rather than being compelled to use them out of fear and dysfunction.

So to be a Master of our own life, we need to own our part in every interaction and relation, in every drama and trauma. We need to drop any and all sense of Victimhood. The Suffering Marytrdom. The Compelled Savior. The Self-Righteous Judge. The Passive/Aggressive Perpetrator. Years ago, I made a dedicated commitment to drop any and all engagement in those dynamics. Let's not waste any more precious energy on that kind of unproductive drama.

Owning how we have showed up, in the past and present NOW. And owning our Self-Agency that we can choose differently moving forward.

We shift our focus away from others. We release expectations around other people. We choose to STOP the manipulation, the passive aggressiveness, the strategizing, the guilt tripping, the blaming, the shaming, the coercion and toxic dependence on others.

We bring our focus constantly and consciously back to WHO WE ARE, and WHO WE CAN BE IN THE PRESENT & FUTURE. We relate to ourselves as THE CAUSE in the matter of own lives. We relate to ourselves as SOURCE of all that is.

Whatever occurs in our inner and outer worlds, we get curious about how we are playing a part in its manifestation, and we rely on only ourselves as the AGENT to change it if desired.

We stop blaming our Mother. Our Father. Our Ex. Men. Women. The Government. Any outside force.

We take the time, space and energy needed to heal our Mother Wound and Father Wound. And everything that has happened to us, we take on that it all happened FOR US, not TO US. And we train ourselves to RELEASE that disempowering dysfunction and embrace Radical Responsibility. Not because what happened didn't matter or wasn't "messed up" or whatever, but rather because we acknowledge ourselves as Masters of our Lives, we value our time and energy, and we choose not to allow draining energy to be in our field anymore.

So instead of identifying with the trauma and wounds that have accumulated over our lifetime, we can investigate them with curiosity and neutrality, and work on dissolving the energy blocks.

When I did the Landmark Forum for the first time in 1998, they talked about how all of us have deep-seated trauma and conditioning from childhood. It's part and parcel of being human and growing up and obtaining an identity, becoming self-aware. In the beginning when we're born, we are like a ball of golden possibility, with no boundaries or barriers. We are everything and everything is us. And then BAM, something happens and it feels bad, and since we have no barriers or boundaries yet, we make it mean that *"I'm bad! I'm wrong! Something's wrong here, so it must be me!"* And we start to feel shame or guilt – which dampens and blocks our light and lifeforce. They say, that shame is when we feel we have violated something good inside ourselves. Guilt is when we feel we have violated something amongst our agreements with others.

After trauma, we then find ways to compensate so that we can avoid feeling that pain ever again. We take on a *"winning formula"* to get through life; we become the class clown, or super smart, or way sexy, or OCD perfectionistic, or stoic -- whatever permutation of qualities we feel will help us survive life. All of this is not a "bad" thing, it can be helpful, but it can also be detrimental and limiting when we feel compelled to be these qualities and there's no choice or spaciousness around it.

This is similar to the Hawaiian concept of the *"Bowl of Light"* that we had mentioned earlier. All of these traumas are rocks that dim our light. And it's really important to take the time to pick the rocks out of our *"Bowl of Light,"* or to break them open to discover the treasure inside.

So part of knowing who you truly are involves healing the old wounds and bringing back the soul fragments that had splintered away from before. It doesn't have to be a very melodramatic or torturous process, it can actually be wonderfully relieving and cathartic. When we remember our true identities as Divine Beings, we don't have to take the wounds so personally, and we can just view them with a neutral mind, with compassion and curiosity.

As an alchemist, transformation is a daily way of life for me, so when I find myself getting triggered or emotionally charged (rarer and rarer these days), I've learned to take a sacred pause, flush it with my full conscious awareness and lean into it, allowing whatever emotion and childlike hurt to get released from it. I have trained myself to get excited about dissolving that "rock" and freeing up more lifeforce as I get to the other side of it. Finding, examining, and transmuting these old wounds are normal for me, as I also hold space for others to do the same on a daily basis.

Of course there are a thousand ways up the mountain, there is no one cookie-cutter way to heal and awaken. I personally enjoyed immersing myself in five years of Landmark Education (doing every course they offered multiple times), two years of Tony Robbins Mastery University and two more years of his Leadership Academy, twelve years of Kundalini Yoga and Sat Nam Rasayan, a year of therapy, a season in the Amazon rainforest studying with shamans and plant medicine, a decade of martial arts and meditation before all that, as well as a year becoming a Facilitator of Family Constellations. I've studied many other modalities as well, as I like to have a wide, diverse range of tools in my toolbox to help my clients.

For me, I loved Landmark and Tony Robbins for the goal-oriented, external success results, and I also love the Kundalini Yoga and Family Constellation work, for their results piercing into the unseen realms, into the unconscious, subconscious, energetic and ancestral realms. Oftentimes, we have taken on vows or limiting beliefs that aren't even ours, that may have been passed onto us from our family line, or taken on by us in order to maintain loyalty or show love to our parents, or even just basically to survive. Other times we have adopted coping mechanisms from childhood trauma, and deeply buried them so that we don't even remember they are there. In my Soul Clearing Sessions, I choose from all these different modalities as I help people uncover, heal and resolve their old wounds and outdated vows.

There is only one of you in all of existence, and it's good for you to get to know yourself, your strengths, your weaknesses, your gifts, your challenges, all of your multidimensional Self. And to transmute anything that blocks your divine light and lifeforce. You are meant to become a Master of your own life. So find what resonates with you and build an extensive support system to help you as you alchemize your stuck energy, remove your rocks, and unfold greater and greater levels of Self Agency and Mastery.

Kundalini Yoga: Ten Bodies System

There are countless different systems and ways of learning about ourselves from different angles; for example, there's Meyers-Briggs, there's Enneagrams, there's Human Design, there's Gene Keys, there's the astrological aspects, etc.

In the Kundalini Yogic Tradition, a human being has Ten Bodies, as well as a Chakra System, etc. We also learn what our Tantric Numerology is so that we can learn about our strengths, weaknesses, gifts and challenges in this lifetime.

For us to go deeper into all this would be a different book, so for now I just want to mention the Ten Bodies here:

Regarding Our Ten Bodies:

"IF YOU UNDERSTAND THAT YOU ARE TEN BODIES, AND YOU ARE AWARE OF THOSE TEN BODIES, AND YOU KEEP THEM IN BALANCE, THE WHOLE UNIVERSE WILL BE IN BALANCE WITH YOU." ~ YOGI BHAJAN

1st   Soul Body
2nd   Negative Mind
3rd   Positive Mind
4th   Neutral Mind
5th   Physical Body
6th   Arcline
7th   Aura
8th   Pranic Body
9th   Subtle Body
10th Radiant Body

What are the Ten Bodies?

The truth is that the human body is made up of ten bodies: the physical body, three mental bodies, and six energy bodies. The eleventh embodiment – when all ten bodies are under your direction – produces a pure state of consciousness when you have the ability to see all events as God's Play and recognize the God in all.

You can visualize your various bodies as layers of clothing, the physical body being the overcoat you wear for a lifetime. We know we have a physical body; we can see it, touch it, and feel it. We also have other bodies that are equally real, if not more so.

-- **More fascinating info on Your Ten Bodies:**

https://www.3ho.org/kundalini-yoga/ten-bodies/characteristics-ten-bodies

[From THE AQUARIAN TEACHER: KRI TEACHER TRAINING LEVEL ONE MANUAL]

Recommendations:

Building Upon Your Personal Sadhana:

So one of the gems that I would like you to get out of the program is a personal daily Sadhana (spiritual practice) that works for you, that you can easily do every day, that feeds and strengthens you, and keeps you grounded and centered.

As we go through this program, I will give you suggestions and recommendations, in creating a basic one that only takes a few minutes a day, but you are free to modify as you wish, for what works best for you.

So far we have a basic structure of:

Sit comfortably, preferably near your altar-meditation area.

Body Scan, Set Intention for your day.

Tune In & Beam Out Intention;

Breath of Fire - Ego Eradicator; (recommended at least 3 minutes)

Meditation to Clear Karma & The Arcline (recommended 3-11 minutes)

Close out with 1-3 Long Sat Nams.

*All of this so far can take less than ten minutes of your day, and can set you up powerfully for your whole day ~

Meditation to Clear Karma and the Arcline:

This video is less than 10 minutes and is a nice, gentle one to do to help leave the past issues behind. I did this one for 31 minutes for

40 days, and though I hated it at times, I felt a substantial lightening each day. With every hand-sweep, I would imagine things I wanted to leave behind and not carry forward into my ideal present. Here the Instructor explains it and does it for 3 minutes:

https://www.youtube.com/watch?v=d8EEiW1_7MI

If it feels helpful to you, then I invite you to add it into your Sadhana for a set amount of days.

They say it takes forty days to make a new habit, so yogis often take on a certain Meditation / Kriya for forty days. But there's plenty of opportunities to choose, create and customize your Sadhana, as we go along, so no pressure. Just something to keep in mind.

Chapter 7:
Embrace Your Emotions

This being human is a guest house.
Every morning a new arrival.

A joy, a depression, a meanness,
some momentary awareness comes
as an unexpected visitor.

Welcome and entertain them all!
Even if they're a crowd of sorrows,
who violently sweep your house
empty of its furniture,
still, treat each guest honorably.
He may be clearing you out
for some new delight.

The dark thought, the shame, the malice,
meet them at the door laughing,
and invite them in.

Be grateful for whoever comes,
because each has been sent
as a guide from beyond.

o Rumi

As a cancer sign, I've always been an extremely emotional person by nature. I've always loved fiercely, often blindly, and sometimes inappropriately! As an empath, I can walk into a room and receive an immediate download of what everyone around me is feeling, wanting, and needing. As a yogi, I can sense people's energetic bodies and auras, as well as knowing the state of their chakras, where they are balanced or not. Oftentimes, I don't even have to see them, I can just tune into them and know. Over the years, I've learned how to manage these gifts so that they are not intrusive or overwhelming.

All of these innate gifts of being human -- including our emotions – are gifts that we just need to learn to master and manage wisely so that they can help us, not harm us.

Back in 2007, after my dark night of the soul and the breakup with my fiancé, I lived in Puerto Rico for a time, and then when we separated, I didn't know where to go. For a while, I went back to Taiwan to be with my roots. My aunt Alice is a wonderfully kind and generous sweet spirit. We loved going to Temples together, that was our shared passion.

One Saturday, Alice took me and her family on a field trip outside of the crowded city streets of Taipei. We drove up in spirals around a beautiful craggy mountain, up to a secret sacred hidden monastery, far away.

There, about a dozen monks in plain brown robes walked about, doing their daily chores and meditations. She chatted to them in Chinese and told them about my heartbreak and my depression. She asked them to give me a *"Spirit Message."*

The monks convened in the altar room. They sat down nonchalantly around a huge wooden table, each with a sheet of parchment. One of the monks went into a trance and started praying and channeling. He would yell out a Chinese character, and one monk would write it down, and then another character and another monk would write it down, until it became a message for me.

After they were done, they each bowed as they left the room and walked away as if it was no big deal.

My aunt read the parchment and looked at me earnestly. She said, *"This is the message that Spirit has for you:* **'MASTER YOUR EMOTIONS AND CULTIVATE WISDOM.'"**

I have always remembered that and cherish that message.

I became determined to do just that and I learned many different methods, some of which I will share with you now:

Proper Relating:

So first and foremost, remember that we are a Divine Multidimensional Being, Spirit Incarnate. That comes first, anchoring into and grounding into our True Core Self. Knowing that we are more than our emotions, more than our passing whims and desires, more than the anger, fear, sadness, shame or guilt that we may be feeling at the time. Then it becomes easier to not overly identify with your emotions (or your thoughts, but that will come next chapter). They are not US, they are just passing through us, with messages for us.

We do this in 3 ways:
Treat Emotions like Weather, like Messengers, and like Small Children.

1)   **Treat Emotions like Weather.**

Observe them neutrally, like a storm passing through.

Allow the emotion to get totally expressed and released.

Sometimes it just needs to express itself, and that will resolve itself on its own, like a storm passing through.

(You wouldn't try to suppress a storm, would you?)

All too often in our society, we suppress, repress, deny, avoid, reject, numb out. We lock away emotions and they get stored and trapped in our body and aura, causing all kinds of stuck energy and disease.

So instead of repressing them, I encourage you to allow their full expression, to find safe ways to process and integrate them, as well as the gifts and wisdom that they carry. I know that oftentimes, in the moment, we cannot fully express them because we are in public or at work, or it would be detrimental, etc. But you can plan to take a sacred pause later on and scream/cry/shake in the car, or the ocean or a pillow, etc.

Allow the holy rage – sadness - fear to pass through you, in a non-harmful way; knowing that they are not You, just needing to come through you, like a storm.

2). Treat Emotions as Messengers.

If you can see everything that happens in life as a gift to bring us more awareness, then emotions are the messengers. They are signifiers, letting us know something that can help us on the trajectory of our life.

Emotions need to be acknowledged, witnessed, listened to, and honored. They are just one aspect of our totality, and have something to tell us. Anger, fear, sadness, shame, guilt – if we could embrace them and honor them as amazing protectors and messengers, then they can become our allies.

For example, in March 2020, when the Covid Pandemic was first coming out, I felt some fear. Instead of denying or suppressing my fear, I allowed myself to sit quietly and feel into the fear. I shone the full light of my conscious awareness on the fear, and worked with it.

I asked it,
"What message do you have for me, my Fear?
What do you need to tell me?
What needs to happen so you can relax?"

The message was:

"*Please go out and get a month's worth of supplies and health supplements for our family.*"

And I answered, "*Ah, okay. Thank you for letting me know. Yes I will do this.*" And I did. And the fear relaxed and joined back into my totality.

3).   Treat Emotions like Small Children.

Another way to relate to emotions in a helpful way is to treat them as if they were a small child. If there was an angry, crying or scared child in front of you, you wouldn't just ignore them or stuff them in a closet or shut them up, correct?

So give your emotions your full presence, and treat them with gentleness, kindness and compassion. Hear them out.

What do they have to tell you?
What do they need from you to feel safe?

Listen to them fully, take the appropriate actions to reassure them, and then allow them to relax because they felt fully seen, heard and acknowledged.

Somatic Method

How to do Soul Clearings on Yourself:

I often provide Soul Clearing Sessions in person or in distance, to help people heal trauma, clear distortion, release the emotion, receive the wisdom and messages, and come back into a resourceful, empowered, soul-centered state.

Each session is tailored to the individual, and comprises of many techniques, but I'd like to share with you one of the key somatic methods I regularly use so that you can do it on yourself or your loved ones.

If I find myself getting triggered now, I pause, I stop.

I get present to myself, I start doing some deep breathing.

I put my hands on my body wherever I feel called
(usually my heart and/or my belly).

I identify – what's the primary emotion I'm feeling?
Is it Anger, Fear, Sadness, Shame or Guilt?

(* Irritation and frustration can be considered Anger; depression and loneliness can be considered Sadness; worry and anxiety can be considered Fear. Shame and Guilt are their own categories and have their own dark frequencies that block light and lifeforce. Often underneath Anger is Sadness. Or if someone is feeling too afraid, I try to bring them into their anger, to feel their holy rage as it can activate their inner fire that way. The emotions are malleable, they often travel together, just different ones at the forefront).

I allow myself to feel the primary emotion fully and completely, even amplifying it.

I shine the light of conscious awareness 100% onto the emotion and the experience.

I think back to when and where else have I felt this way.

I allow my mind to light upon it like watching a trailer for a movie.
All the times that I felt this way, and where it came from, and with who, allowing myself to feel all of it, to go deeper and heal it at a root level, a causal level.

Going back in memory to the very first times I felt this and where it came from.

And I encourage myself to keep feeling it fully, even amplifying and magnifying it.

As I continue to breathe deep and shine the conscious light of awareness, 100% on what I'm feeling and I allow it to be there in all its fullness.

I witness it like watching a lightning storm pass through.

I breathe deep and allow the breath to move the energy.

I might feel tingling or sensations in the body, that's okay.

Many people are very mental and don't allow themselves to feel things fully or be so deeply in their bodies. For these people that often get stuck in the mind and the rationalizing, it can be helpful to ask the following questions:

Ok, this emotion in your body, let me ask you this:

What color is it?
What shape is it?
Density?

Temperature?

Size?

How old is it?

If it had a message what would it tell me?

What else?

What else?

What would it want me to do to assuage its emotion?

What would allow it to relax and be put to rest?

OK tell it you got the message and you will do it.

Thank it, honor it for its message.

See it as one aspect of your totality, and allow it to join in with the rest of your team...

(* There's more that happens in a Soul Clearing Session, but this is one of the basic and common techniques that you can do on your own to help yourself. We usually work on clearing one to three main issues in a 60-90 minute session.)

One of my clients went through this series of questions with her angry toddler, and the child externalized a red spiky ball as big as her fist, inside her belly. She kept bringing breath, presence, and awareness to it until it dissolved and disappeared. So this is a good, simple method that you can share with your loved ones as well.

Recommendations:

Kundalini Yoga for Emotional Balance:

Kundalini Yoga offers many ways to balance, release and master emotions. Here are some of my favorites:

Alternate Nostril Breathing
For an easy way to calm down, I usually do this one:
https://www.3ho.org/alternate-nostril-breathing

Meditation for Emotional Balance
https://www.3ho.org/3ho-lifestyle/health-and-healing/kundalini-yoga-emotional-balance

Fists of Fury
This is one of my favorite quick fixes, you can do this for three minutes to release anger, depression, frustration, and overwhelm.
https://rama-tv.com/wp-content/uploads/2016/09/Fists-of-Anger.pdf

RA MA DA SA Healing Meditation:

Sit comfortably in easy pose (cross-legged).

Bring your hands palm up, right above your thighs, elbows comfortably resting against your sides.

In your mind's eye, see your little inner child.

Bathe them in golden healing light.

Make them small, seat them on a golden throne, and place them in your heart.

We will be chanting the mantra: "RA MA DA SA, SA SAY SO HUNG"

The mantra means: *"The Sun, The Moon, The Earth, Infinity -- I Am That"*

Envision that you are singing a Healing Lullaby to soothe and comfort your inner child.

And now click on this link below, and chant along --

https://www.youtube.com/watch?v=YQrs9zlOW1U

(Snatam Kaur's version of this mantra is so nice, sometimes I play it in the background whenever I need a healing, calming vibration).

Chapter 8: Neutralize Your Mind – Aligning with Infinite Wisdom

"The mind is a wonderful servant, but a terrible master."
– Robin Sharma

So Dear One, now we move into Mastery of the Mind. As we've discussed before, once we reclaim our true identity as Spirit Incarnate, and place our Soul Self in the driver's seat of our lives, then we can relate to everything else in its proper perspective. We can then stop overidentifying with our past history, our emotions -- and now also from our mind.

Earlier, we discussed how in the Kundalini yogic tradition, we have Ten Bodies, and Three Minds. The three minds are Positive, Negative, and Neutral. None is better than the other, we actually need to cultivate each of them to be strong and healthy, and then essentially operate and make decisions from the Neutral Mind. Let's delve deeper into them now, one by one:

The Positive (Expansive) Mind

The Positive Mind sees the positive aspects of all situations and beings. It is expansive and allows resources in. It gives you a strong will and allows you to use your power easily and humbly. It makes you naturally playful and optimistic and makes your communication strong and direct.

If the Positive Mind is weak, you can be overwhelmed by the input of your Negative Mind which can be depressing and paralyzing. You may feel angry and intolerant or hesitate to use your own power, because you are afraid of the responsibility it brings. If the Positive Mind is overactive and not balanced with a strong Negative and Neutral Mind, then you might ignore risks, overgive and allow people to take advantage of you.

Key Concepts: Equality, Optimism

Key Questions: Am I open to all possibilities that life has to offer? Do I let these into my life?

Key to Balance: Strengthen the navel point. Increase your self-esteem. Use positive affirmations. Strengthen the Negative and Neutral Minds to balance.

Tips on Developing the Positive Mind

Adopt Blessed Perception & Apply a Miracle Mindset

Another key way to strengthen the Positive Mind is by adopting blessed perception and apply a miracle mindset. Your current default mindset can be seen as the sum of your parents, close friends, societal conditioning – and it's usually fear and judgment based and not very empowering. There are so many different kinds of mindsets we can take on to view the world, and you don't have to keep the ones that you were raised with. All the thoughts and beliefs we have about money, relationships, sex, men, women, morality, business, the world, etc. were mostly not consciously chosen, they are like a pair of dirty sunglasses that we inherited that color our worldview and obscure our true vision. So rather than blindly accepting our default mindset, I am inviting you to take off that pair of dirty sunglasses, and consciously adopt a clean, clear mindset that empowers you.

So I invite you to adopt blessed perception and apply a miracle mindset – the idea that anything and everything that ever happens and occurs to you, is a total blessing for your benefit, and that miracles and grace are normal everyday occurrences. Allow that to be the starting point from which you view the world. From there, you then develop the practice of actively looking, claiming and seeking out how everything that happens is actually a blessing of some kind, how everything is actually always working out in your favor, whether you can see it yet or not.

So let's invite grace and miracles to have a place in your life. If you find this challenging in a certain situation, then perhaps you can just relate to it as "a blessing in disguise," as we cultivate trust and faith in Life and the Ways of the Universe, rather than our limited human sight or agendas.

Quantum Questions

One of the ways to develop this practice is by asking *"Quantum Questions."* The mind likes to gnaw on questions, so with this process, we can give it what it wants, but we lead and direct it by asking high quality, empowering questions.

For example, when something happens that may seem "negative," instead of asking myself, *"Why is this happening to me,"* instead we can ask ourselves questions such as:

Why is this happening FOR me?
How is this blessing me?
How is this actually awesome?
How is this a miracle?
What are the good aspects?
If I take a wider viewpoint, how does this weave into the greater tapestry of blessings?
What infinite possibilities become available to me now?

Quantum Questions are not meant to really be answered, they are meant to be asked and allowed to resound in your Being, and to redirect your mind and focus back to one of positive blessings.

Negative (Protective) Mind

The Negative Mind helps you with the gifts of containment, discernment, and discipline. It gives you patience to be obedient to your own inner guidance. It allows you to see the possible risks in a situation and to set good boundaries for yourself.

If your Negative Mind is underdeveloped, your longing to belong can cause you to get into inappropriate self-destructive relationships because you are over-influenced by others; you aren't contained enough in your own center. If your Negative Mind is overactive and too fearful and protective, then you can be very pessimistic, self-sabotaging and often stopping the blessings of life from coming to you. You would need to balance it out by strengthening the Positive Mind and the Neutral Mind.

Key Concepts: Discipline, Discernment, Containment, Obedience

Key Questions: Where's the danger in a situation? What do I need to consider?

Key to Balance: Value your discipline. Develop conscious relationships of integrity. Strengthen the Positive and Neutral Minds to balance.

Tips on Developing the Negative Mind

Get used to tallying the pros and cons of something, and listening to and honoring your divine intuition and your "gut feelings." From these signals, create and honor your strong boundaries. Value your time, space, energy and Self more and more. Give up people pleasing and refuse to be manipulated. Create and enforce good boundaries with others, and learn how to communicate them clearly and well so that all can be truly honored.

A 10 Day Challenge

I invite you to pay attention to your words and thoughts closely. Oftentimes, we're unaware that we project or perpetuate negativity. Once you've become aware of patterns of negativity, see if you can take a ten-day challenge and go without any negative words or thoughts for that time period.

Every time the phrases "I can't" or "I don't like" pop into your head, dismiss them. Begin negating the negative. In my mind, I sometimes, say "Cancel Clear" and imagine a big "X" on something. For each negative, see if you can find a way to turn it into a positive.

Another step you can take is to begin to differentiate between pain and discomfort, and eliminate the negativity associated with discomfort. If you're feeling true physical pain, it's an indication that something is wrong and must be corrected. But discomfort—moving against resistance, stretching muscles that haven't been used, or developing awareness that is new to us—allows us to grow. Can you transform the "I can't" mantra to "Sat Nam," to give you the strength to keep up?

Mantra to Reverse Negativity

And now I leave you with one of my favorite mantras, that reverses negativity. It's also called the "Magic Mantra," and whenever I feel like I'm spiraling down into negativity, I stop and play this mantra instead. The mantra is:

EK ONG KAAR, SAT GUR PRASAAD, SAT GUR PRASAAD, EK ONG KAR

When chanted at least five times, it acts as a "gudtkaa" – a lever to reverse negative energy to positive. (Sat Kirin Kaur has a beautiful version of it in her album "Lightness of Being," which can be found on Spirit Voyage website.)

Neutral (Meditative) Mind

The Neutral or Meditative Mind is the ultimate "win-win" mentality. From here you look at the whole play of life with compassion. The Neutral Mind evaluates the input of your Negative and Positive Minds (and the rest of the Ten Bodies as well) and gives you guidance quickly. It is a very intuitive vantage point and allows you to access your Soul.

If your Neutral Mind is weak, you may have a hard time making decisions. You'll have the habit of feeling victimized by life because you don't know how to integrate your experiences and find meaning in them. You may have a hard time seeing beyond the polarities of life on Earth and tuning into the great cosmic scheme of things.

The neutral mind is like a scale. Its attributes are compassion, service, and balance. It balances and weighs the information being offered to it by the positive mind (what could go right?) and the negative mind (what could go wrong?). It rises above agenda and the details of the world to give a more neutral, yet compassionate determination of your best path. Strong neutral minds can evaluate and determine the best course within nine seconds. A weak neutral mind means that you are at the mercy of the dueling positive and negative minds. You will be changeable, have trouble making up your mind, get involved in a mental war with yourself, and be at the mercy of a roller coaster of emotions. The neutral mind slows that process down and allows you to come from an objective, compassionate, and devotional place.

One of the biggest gifts of the neutral mind is that it allows you to see everything that has happened to you (good or bad) in terms of blessings and gifts. Obstacles become opportunities, and you can see the blessings in all. If you are stuck in a place of grief and sadness with a "why me?" mentality, you could benefit from strengthening the Neutral Mind.

Key Qualities: Service, Compassion, Integration, Balance

Key Questions: Do I allow myself to perceive and act upon inner wisdom?

Tips on Developing the Neutral Mind

Establish a regular meditation practice. Meditation trains the mind towards equanimity – a calm centeredness that does not react wildly to stimuli. Meditation will help you to align yourself with Infinite Wisdom, develop the Frontal Lobe, and stimulate the pineal and pituitary glands – which help to develop your intuition, your clarity of vision, and your psychic perceptions.

You can also master the mind, using the tool of Mantra. Whenever I find my mind being overactive ("monkey mind") or over negative, I allow it be and I play mantras in the background to reverse that negativity and attune it to a higher chosen frequency.

The Unconscious, Subconscious, Conscious and Supra Conscious Minds:

Besides the Positive, Negative and Neutral Minds; let's take a look at another angle – the Unconscious, Subconscious, Conscious and Super Conscious Minds.

Yogi Bhajan explains it like this:

"When you speak unconsciously, you represent your emotions, your feelings, your neuroses, your handicaps, your shortcomings, and your insecurities.

When you speak subconsciously, you are a con-person, you are a thief, you are a cheat, you manipulate, you are dishonest. All you want is to win the moment or impress the moment. Such people are never true to a bigger picture; they are never real in their lives.

When you speak consciously, that which you speak about happens.

When you speak supra-consciously from the supreme self of you, that becomes the guiding line for the Universe. Then the akashic record has to move with that angle."

So be aware of which mind you are dwelling in and speaking from. There are many ways to make what's unconscious conscious and to retrain the subconscious mind. One of my favorite things to teach in Kundalini Yoga is an advanced, intense set of kriya and breathwork called "Rebirthing." It clears the subconscious, dumps the garbage, and heals childhood wounds. Yogi Bhajan said "the subconscious is the storehouse of misery." It's like a computer system that needs to get rebooted, cleared, and dumped on a regular basis.

Besides Yoga, I also like to listen to mantras 24/7, as well as delta/theta frequencies at night to reprogram my subconscious mind towards values of my choosing. Hypnosis also works. I also highly recommend one of my mentors, Jason Christoff's work – he is a self-sabotage coach and Truth Teller and helps people to wake up out of their old childhood conditioning and unconscious programming to awaken their full potential. Without doing this inner work, you may never get what you want in life, as your subconscious will find ways to sabotage your success. So do some research and find which methods resonate with you.

Recommended

The One Minute Breath:

This is a great and easy practice to do to calm the mind and relieve anxiety.

In essence, the practice is to:

Inhale for 20 seconds, Hold for 20 seconds, Exhale for 20 seconds.

But start off with 5 - 5 - 5.

Work your way up as you can.

Detailed info and instructions here:

https://www.3ho.org/kundalini-yoga/pranayam/one-minute-breath

Ten Day Fast from Negativity

As mentioned earlier, go on a 10 Day Fast from speaking negativity, consciously catching yourself whenever you find yourself grumbling, criticizing, judging yourself / others / situations in a negative light.

Instead, notice that, stop, and practice asking yourself Quantum Questions to help you find the blessings (sometimes in disguise) in and every situation for 10 days. (If you feel this is beneficial to you, consider extending this to 21 or 40 days.)

Chapter 9: Illuminate Your Speech, Cultivating Conscious Communication

Dear One, now that you are exercising more mastery over your Multidimensional Self, your emotions and your thoughts, the next step is to cultivate mastery with the expression of these as embodied in your Spoken Word. Your Word is one of your birthright gifts, it's one of your most powerful God given tools, and is crucial for creating your ideal reality and manifesting your will on Earth.

For many people, communication consists of a limited scope and low vibration. A lot of it what people call communicating is actually -- strategizing, manipulating, avoiding, defending, blaming, shaming, judging, surviving, and just describing. I've known people who just describe their day, the weather, their neuroses, their complaints about others and gossip all day long. All this low vibe communication leaves people at the effect of their world, with little agency.

But what if you could communicate on a higher level; and speak and listen in a way that evoked Power, Possibility, Freedom and Richness for both you and others?

This would be Conscious Languaging and Communication, which is an art form, a science, and a crucial skill set. It is the access to greater Freedom, Power, Prosperity, Manifestation, as well as Intimacy and Authentic Relating, Magic and so much more. I've studied this field extensively, mainly from the lens of Landmark Education, Tony Robbins, and also Kundalini Yoga, and will be sharing six key concepts with you now.

- 1st Concept –

Communication as Talking, Speaking, Dialoguing
– what's the difference?
I vs We -- Talk to Conquer vs Talk to Connect?

- 2nd Concept –

What's driving the communication?
What's underneath, yours and theirs?
Unmet need? Get it / Fix it?
(Validation / Solutions?)

- 3rd Concept –

Which Chakra are you speaking from?

- 4th Concept –

Embracing the Power of the Generative Word, With Invocation, Incantation, Mantras, Vows

- 5th Concept –

The Power of Deep Listening, Presence & Acknowledgment

First Concept

According to Yogi Bhajan, there are three main ways to communicating - Talking, Speaking, Dialoguing. Let's expound on the differences:

The first mode is Talking. Have you ever been just talked at? Where it's as if it doesn't even matter if the listener is there or not? So this first mode is like when someone is just spewing their wants, needs and agenda on someone else; with no consideration of if it's landing, how it's landing or what's happening in the others' world. It can be a painful experience, like the conqueror and conquered; all about "I", instead of "We."

The second mode is Speaking. This is when both parties have a basic relay, and they can basically understand each other. There is a We. It can be very transactional, can be neutral, can be positive.

And then there's the third mode, which is creating Dialogue. Yogi Bhajan describes Dialogue as *"that sweet zone when two people are communicating in the same frequency, at the same moment, with the same passion, same compassion, same individuality and identity...At a high level, it's like an intercourse where it feels like communication is happening very effortlessly, gracefully, like there's a flow and harmony. Where there's a merge of intelligence and consciousness, heart and mind meeting."* There's an experience of oneness, grace, and time disappearing.

So check in when you are communicating, and see if you are "talking to conquer" or "talking to cultivate relationship and mutuality"? Is it all about "I" or "We"? Are you talking with passion to make your point, or compassion, to understand their side as well and meet them in mutuality?

Second Concept

Here, we look at -- What's driving the communication? What's beyond the words, and underneath it, both yours and theirs? I invite you to sensitize yourself to hear what's the underlying communication and deeper urge beyond the words?

For example -- one of the first things you can do is ask them or yourself – WAIT – is this a "Get it" or a "Fix it"? Do you just want to just feel heard -- in which case, ideally, the other would just listen with no interruption, and perhaps mirror back exactly what was said? Or do you want help in fixing something -- in which case, you welcome advice and suggestions? A lot of couples get into problems because oftentimes women just want to talk and feel heard, while men tend to hear something and want to fix it right away. So first, discern or ask, if something is a "Get it / Fix it"?

Also, see if you can feel into what is the greater unmet need they are wanting, in general? Do they want to feel validated? Acknowledged? Seen? Heard? Understood? Appreciated? Guided? Comforted? Reassured? Loved?

What is it?

For example, someone could be saying, "Hey honey, did you take the trash out? How was your day? Do you want something to eat? How do you want your eggs cooked? Etc." -- while underneath all their communications, they could actually be constantly asking you – "Do you love me? Am I okay?" Or even "I can't stand you." Etc. So feel into what's beyond the words.

In my 20's, I was such a people pleaser, and when I took some Communication Courses at Landmark Education, we did an exercise where all of us looked at what was underneath our surface words. I saw that underneath, I was unconsciously asking: "Am I okay? Am I safe? Are you going to hurt me? What do I need to do so you like and accept me and thus, don't hurt me?" We then all walked around the room, bumping into each other and saying our sentences like these, and saw that our fellow humans have these insecure statements underneath their words also. We were able to laugh and gain some spaciousness and freedom around this, and move forward. Whenever we bring the unconscious to light, we gain a little more freedom and agency around the issue.

So sensitize yourself to find out what is underneath your own communication, and also what is underneath those you interact with?

And respond from there, rather than just the surface.

Third Concept

Which Chakra are you/ they speaking from? And which mind? So chakras are like energy hubs in the body, and each one has a certain focus and theme. A brief summary:

ROOT – Safety, security, survival

SACRUM – passion, creativity, sexuality

SOLAR PLEXUS – mastery, self-agency, willpower

HEART – loving, forgiving, giving, receiving

THROAT – speaking one's truth, manifesting one's word

THIRD EYE – intuition, wisdom

CROWN – connection with Source, divinity

So when you're speaking or listening to others, start paying attention to which chakra you / they are speaking from, and also notice if it's coming from a strengthened or a weakened place. Every chakra has a positive, strengthened attribute as well as a negative, weakened attribute. I'll give some (somewhat funny) examples of these:

ROOT

Positive: *"I feel safe and secure. We always have enough."*

Negative: *"Oh no, we're broke! How are we going to survive?"*

SACRUM

Positive: *"I am loving the projects that I am cultivating! And my juicy partner!*

Negative: *"I don't care.. Hey baby, what's your number?"*

SOLAR PLEXUS

Positive: *"I am my own master. I choose yes or no."*

Negative: *"I don't think I can, don't we have to ask someone else?"*

HEART

Positive: *"I love and forgive. I give and receive."*

Negative: *"What's wrong with you? I'll never forgive you."*

THROAT

Positive: *"I can speak my Truth, I can sing my song, I can manifest my Word!"*

Negative: (clears throat) *"….Umm… I don't know what to say.."*

THIRD EYE

Positive: *"Ah yes I know. I trust and honor my divine Intuition."*

Negative: *"I have no idea what to do. I feel so lost."*

CROWN

Positive: *"I feel guided, blessed, connected with the Universe."*

Negative: *"I am all alone. Life is dark and scary."*

So can you begin to see how peoples' speech can be coming from different chakras? And expressing from the positive / negative attributes?

And so now I invite you to sensitize yourself and practice listening beyond the words, feeling into which chakra you as well as others may be speaking from. And – when you find yourself speaking in the negative, weak attribute of a chakra, I invite you to consciously practice flipping it to the positive side of the chakra.

Another practice you can do, is to switch which chakra you are speaking from. For example – when I first began teaching Kundalini Yoga, I used to always teach strongly from my HEART chakra, so my classes were always warm, nurturing and overflowing with love. No one wanted to leave the love fest! That was all great, but the downside of that was that it indulged my shadow aspects as a people pleaser and over emphasized me being loved and admired.

As I continued to mature and develop as a teacher, I learned to teach from my other chakras as well – from my Navel Point, from my Solar Plexus, from my Third Eye, etc. The classes became less about me making sure my students feel good and became more about being able to deliver the message – being able to hold and guide people through a deep arc of transformation – which isn't always pleasant!

When I started speaking and teaching from the full, positive range of all of my chakras more, people felt they could trust me more, as I could bring the full rainbow spectrum to the table as I guided people to grow thru hardship, difficulty, tough love and wise compassion as well as with the Unconditional Love. So be aware of where you and others are directing your communication from, and practice shifting to different energy centers as appropriate.

(In addition, here's a little tip, if you want to impact/influence someone, you can project your frequency strongly from your third eye point into theirs…

That's another reason why it's good to get used to setting your frequency and intention and beaming it out from your third eye point. Because the one with the stronger frequency will generally "win.")

Fourth Concept

This brings us to the 4th point -- Embracing the Power of the Generative Word. This kind of language is the most powerful, magical, and GODLY, as it creates a new reality from nothing. So rather than just survive or describe one's neurosis, or be at the effect of the world around them, Generative Speech takes on a godly quality and creates a new reality.

Examples of this include:
Declarations, Invocations, Incantations, Mantras, Vows.

So here are some more specific examples of each one, some may overlap.

Declarations

Declarations are generative language that call forth something from nothing. In the first line of the first book of the Bible – Genesis -- God said, *"Let there be Light."* And Light came across the land. Another common declaration we all know is: *"I now pronounce you Husband and Wife"* -- and a whole new reality then opens up for that couple.

Invocations

Invocations call upon and evoke from the unseen realm. When we chant the Adi Mantra (ONG NAMO GURU DEV NAMO), we are invoking infinite wisdom to be present. In many indigenous cultures, they begin their ceremonies by opening up sacred space with calling upon the Four Directions. Another example of an invocation is a Christian saying something like - *"I call upon the power of the Holy Spirit to heal this person now!"*

Incantations

Incantations are like prayers or mantras charged up with passion, emotional intensity and focus. They are helpful in reprogramming the subconscious mind. At the Tony Robbins' events, they had a certain Incantation that we chanted several times a day with fervor and conviction. It was:

"Now I am the voice
I will lead, not follow
I will create, not destroy
I will believe, not doubt
I am a force for good
Set a new standard
Step up!"

Mantras

We've mentioned the power of Mantras a few times now. I pretty much listen to mantras 24/7. For me, they are like spells, like "white magic" (magic used for beneficial good purposes). Exalted frequencies that go beyond and reach into another dimension. There are thousands of mantras, in countless traditions. Some common ones in Kundalini Yoga are:

ONG NAMO GURU DEVA NAMO - invokes Wisdom & Guidance
The Mangalan Charan - invokes Protection
RA MA DA SA - invokes Healing
SAT NAM - invokes Truth
BAHOTA KARAM – invokes prosperity (aka "the Millionaire Mantra")
Etc.

But it doesn't need to be fancy or in a different language. One of the most powerful mantras ever is simply -- "Thank You." If one can just say "thank you, thank you," no matter what is happening in life, miracles can happen. The frequency of gratitude is one of the highest possible.

Vows

Vows are like sacred, inviolable promises that definitively shape one's reality. They are one of my favorite examples of generative language, partly because they are so rarely used in everyday life. Besides marriage vows, do you ever recall using a vow? When I do Soul Clearings on people, we often times will spotlight old, unconscious, limiting vows; release them, and then declare new amazing, empowering ones.

So as mentioned earlier, a common conscious vow is "*I take you to be my Husband/Wife.*" However, we have all made all kinds of unconscious vows that we oftentimes don't even remember or are unaware of, yet they affect us greatly. For example, a heartbroken person might vow "to never love again," or a person growing up in poverty might vow to "get rich no matter what it takes." These strong promises change the course of their life.

Last weekend, one of my clients came for a Private Healing Retreat and Soul Clearing with me at my Magical Lava Temple. There, we uncovered some old, disempowering vows like – "*I vow to always be the good girl. I vow to put everyone else first. I vow to serve the men in my life.*" Unfortunately, this led to a lifetime of pain, martyrdom, suppressed rage and three expensive divorces.

I said, *"no wonder you can't have more abundance in your life, why would the Universe grant you more wealth when your partners keep stealing it from you? Which leads to betrayal and heartache and even more pain? You can't have more wealth until you can hold and manage it well."*

So we cleared out the old wounds, uprooted and broke the old vows, and activated her solar plexus so that she would be able to create healthy boundaries and practice greater self-agency.

We then stood barefeet on the lava facing the volcano, and I guided her to make some new vows, with me, God and Pele as witnesses.

She proclaimed:

"I VOW to cherish & protect my Self, my Body, my Heart, my Soul, my Mind, my Health, my Wealth ~

I VOW to cherish & protect my Children, my Inner Child, my Capacities, my Creativity ~

I VOW to be a good Steward & Sovereign for all these blessings, & we welcome & invite more ~

And so it is!"

Whenever one feels compelled, compulsive, or powerless around a given situation, that is a strong hint that you may be under the effect of an outdated or unconscious vow. Again, that's an opportunity to bring consciousness to the area and transform it, and open up more freedom, power and blessings to come.

So let me ask you -- what would your life would look like if you used more of this High Caliber, High Quality of Communication in your daily life?

Instead of just using words to describe your day, your partner, your job, your complaints, etc.; which traps you into a default autopilot existence where you are a victim and at the effect of the world -- what if you wielded the power of your Word to create the Reality you daily step into? To declare who you are and what you stand for in your lifetime? To invoke help and protection from unseen legions of angels, to use incantations to program your subconscious mind to work FOR you, not against you? To make worthy vows that empower you and open up new blessings, instead of limiting you? *"Let there be light! Let there be Love! Let there be Abundance! May it be so!"*

When I was immersed in Landmark Education, we practiced this generative power of the word constantly. Every day we declared new possibilities of who we are and could be. For example, at the courses, when it was time to introduce ourselves, we would stand up on stage in front of sometimes hundreds of people – and instead of saying our names, where we're from, or such -- we would declare – *"Who I am is the Possibility of being Unconditional Love, Wisdom and Compassion!"* or *"Who I am is the Possibility of Being an Enlightened World that works for everyone!"* And we would end it with *"And that is who I am!"*

We got comfortable generating and trying on new possibilities all the time, and trafficking in these realms of manifestation 24/7. We consciously created every aspect of our lives, we declared how much money we would make, we made vows to our partners of who we would be for them, we generated new possibilities for ourselves and our lives on a daily basis.

We were training ourselves to see our Word as sacred and inviolable, and to not only KEEP our word, but to BE our Word. To stake our whole life on it. Imagine being so in integrity with your Word that when you say *"I will make $50k a month,"* that it has no choice but to appear (which it did). Or *"I will travel to the Amazon by myself and study with Shamans"* (which I did) or *"I will write a book in 9 weeks"* (which I did) and just make it happen because you have trained yourself and your environment to know yourself as your Word.

I learned to be so in integrity and so rigorous with my word that I trained myself and the environment to manifest whatever I spoke into existence. To speak out a new possibility like throwing a hat over a fence, and then mobilizing all one's resources to keep one's word no matter what. Did we always succeed? Of course not. But it was like building a muscle, and with every breakdown, we would leap forward into a new breakthrough.

So I invite you to become very conscious of your speech and rigorous with your word. The words that follow "I AM" define you. So be mindful of what you tell yourself internally as well as speak aloud.

Fifth Concept

Here, we go beyond the Spoken Word, to the power of Deep Listening and Presence. It doesn't matter how eloquent and articulate you are, words are just words, if you don't potentiate them, if you don't cultivate the power of presence and truth behind them. For example, when people say "talk is cheap," I would refute and say no, our Word is sacred, it's more like "people often cheapen talk." But not us!

So besides verbal communication, I invite you to cultivate your powers of deep listening and presence. Most people don't really listen; they maybe half-listen, while in their head they are already figuring out their response, or perhaps the counter point they want to make. This actually prevents intimacy. The person never feels truly heard and understood, so generally, their complaint or issue will just persist.

In my different trainings, I learned how to empty my mind, release any ego or agendas, and to just be present with nothing to prove and nothing to add or fix. I also learned to listen so deeply that people could feel truly heard, perhaps for the first time, and even feel healed, clearer, and lighter. I learned to listen to a complaint so deeply, that it disappears.

Enjoy the Silence

One of the most impactful experiences in my lifetime was doing a Ten-Day Silent Retreat at a convent in France during college. Twenty of us all walking around a beautiful nunnery, upholding silence. We learned to sit and let the mud settle, to feel each other's beingness, to emanate kindness through our eyes, to communicate without words. We strengthened our connection to Spirit, as we learned to listen deeply to our own internal Soul Voice.

As a householder with business, guests, clients, child, etc., I have carried this wisdom into my life by practicing intentional silence and mindful speech even while going about the busyness of my daily life. I am committed to avoid drama and gossip; and I choose to only hold space for uplifting or transformational conversations. If I have a complaint, I make it a committed complaint, where I vent out for a limited time and with the intention of transforming it and resolving it. If I have a complaint about someone, I am committed to talking about it with them directly, rather than gossip. When relating with others, I try to practice listening more than speaking, listening to and feeling into what's behind the words, and always reaching for what treasure can be shared in this dialogue.

Conscious Communication is an art, a science and a crucial skillset. So I invite you to practice Silence and Mindful Speech as much as possible. Consider doing a ten day fast from speaking if you can. Sensitize yourself to what is unseen, unsaid and underneath. If you must speak, allow the speech to be minimal, mindful, and come from Truth and your Heart. Imagine that every block of silence is like a bar of gold, and every mindful word is like a gem that you give to someone. Allow your days to be filled with gold and gems. Allow your speech to gain greater weight, impact and power as it potentiates in the vessel of silence.

Commit to never speak limitation (yours or others) into your present or future again. (You can say *"I used to be bad at math,"* or *"Historically, I felt scared about that"* but don't speak any limitation into your present or future ever again). Commit to cherish and refine the power of your Word.

Recommended

Vows

Examine where you feel stuck, limited, trapped, compulsive.

Inquire into if there is an old vow keeping your limitations in place.

Consciously break it and create a new vow.

Acknowledgement Exercise

We can generally assume that most people are starving for true acknowledgement. One of the five key Love Languages is "Words of Affirmation," and one of my favorite exercises to do in my workshops is to pair people up and allow each person to be completely acknowledged. (This is an awesome exercise to do with your partner or children at home too.)

Full Directions are here:

http://theradiantlotus.org/acknowledgement-exercise/

(* In doing these exercises, I hope you can see that to listen deeply, actively and with full presence is one of the greatest gifts you can give someone and can build so much connection and intimacy.

Please practice this quality more and more in your life, and especially with your loved ones. Grant them this gift. Be generous with your listening and your presence. Praise them, adore them, acknowledge them often. It doesn't matter if they think you're weird or don't return the favor at first. You are the leader, you need to set the example first. Create the love-filled reality you want to live in and share. See the magic and blessings that develop over time because of your courage and generosity.

Chapter 10: X.
Make Your Mark, Claim Your Crown & Master Your Domain

Our deepest fear is not that we are inadequate.
Our deepest fear is that we are powerful beyond measure.
It is our light, not our darkness
That most frightens us.

We ask ourselves
Who am I to be brilliant, gorgeous, talented, fabulous?
Actually, who are you not to be?
You are a child of God.

Your playing small
Does not serve the world.
There's nothing enlightened about shrinking
So that other people won't feel insecure around you.

We are all meant to shine,
As children do.
We were born to make manifest
The glory of God that is within us.

It's not just in some of us;
It's in everyone.

And as we let our own light shine,
We unconsciously give other people permission to do the same.
As we're liberated from our own fear,
Our presence automatically liberates others.

■ Marianne Williamson

Dear One, you have done so well in getting this far. You have done some inner work to gain inner self mastery, and you can now begin to transfer that focus and power to align and affect your outer reality. Everything always begins from within. If you don't have that inner consciousness and vision first, that internal guidance system, then you would be easily manipulated and a slave at the whim of everyone else's agendas. You must have a strong core and Soul-centered inner compass, so that you can then direct and create your ideal blessed life.

So instead of being a meat suit in a machine, a slave to the masses, please begin to see and treat yourself not only as Spirit Incarnate, but also as a King or Queen walking upon this earth. It's time for you to claim your Sovereignty and create your King/Queendom around you, for the benefit of all.

I know our neuroses and insecurities may start to rear their ugly heads and ask – *"Who am I to be a King/Queen? Am I worthy? Am I enough? Will I lose love if I step up into this?"*

But we are all meant to rise up and be our best Self. It doesn't mean being egotistical and arrogant. It doesn't mean being a tyrant or thinking that we are better than anyone else. We all have this capacity and opportunity. It simply means honoring this precious life and the gifts we have been given and vowing to be a good steward of it all. It means making the most of our lives and creating goodness around us for the benefit of all those in our orbit.

For decades, I did not embrace all the fullness and glory of who I truly am. I was acting like a victim and a martyr, I put everyone else first, I let others have their way with me, abuse me and dictate my life. It resulted in a lot of pain, drama and trauma for no good result. Thankfully, I also spent decades de-conditioning myself from all these toxic disempowering patterns and learning to rise up and answer to my Highest Self as well as become a Lighthouse for others.

My spiritual name is Jade Rajbir Kaur. I was named after Jade Mountain, the highest peak in northeast Asia. "Rajbir Kaur" means "Princess of God who embodies Royal Courage." I now know that I am a Daughter of Mountains and a Lioness of God. I commit to be a Master and a Queen in my lifetime. I accept and embrace these mantles, and I act accordingly. And now, I invite you to rise into your own fullness as well.

I remember sitting at my first Grandfather Ceremony in a small midtown Manhattan apartment back in 2008. It was my first time, and I didn't know anyone in the intimate circle of five that had gathered in a little room. Spirit had guided me to be there so I answered the call. The host was a beautiful woman with dark hair and dark eyes, and she passed around a bowl of the San Pedro plant medicine for us to ingest, and the Guyanese Shaman started shaking a rattle and singing icaros (medicine songs). I felt a different consciousness start to emerge within me, it was the spirit of San Pedro. It felt like the most gentle, kind, grandfatherly energy was dwelling within me and beaming love at me. It felt like he was bolstering my spine with a column of white light, gently correcting my energetic posture.

"It's okay, dear. We love you. Sit upright and straight. Take up space," he seemed to say. As the ceremony went on, the Grandfather Spirit continued to gently work on me and dialogue with my soul.

"It's okay. You're okay. Make your prayers, command your space. You've done this all before, dear; and it's time now to do it again. Now sing your songs," he urged.

The Shaman had just finished a long, haunting icaro and was preparing for the next one. Everyone had been sitting back silently with their eyes closed, when I suddenly spoke up and asked, *"Excuse me, is it okay if I sing a song?"* They all stared at me speechless, and then the Shaman said, *"Yes, sure, please do."* To everyone's surprise (mine included), I began to sing a Christian hymn from my heart.

Lead me, Lord
Lead me in your Righteousness
Make your way plain, before my face
For it is you, Lord
You, Lord, only
Who makest me dwell in safety ~

There was a moment of silence, and then warm smiles and nods of approval. *"Thank you so much, Jade. What a gift. Please, who else feels called to sing? Let's go in a circle,"* said the Shaman.

Each person rose up, took up space and sang their song. It was a magical, heartfelt night and we all felt like beloved friends, giddy schoolkids, and empowered Lightwarriors. Grandfather San Pedro dwelled with us, smiling and beaming love. I felt the presence of my ancestors, my beneficent unseen guides. They did not want me to be timid or shy or have false modesty; they also encouraged me to rise up, command my space, and let my voice be heard.

After that, I ended up becoming great friends with the host Kunana, which meant "Lady of Light," and I ended up accompanying the Shaman as "Fire Keeper" to other ceremonies as well. I hosted ceremonies for him in my SoHo basement several times and again, we enjoyed more magic, healing, heartfelt nights. I greatly respect and appreciate plant medicine for the gifts that they can bring us, and I do feel that they can be of great benefit, when guided by an experienced Facilitator, conducted in a safe container, and with the right protocols and context.

Kundalini Yoga can also help us to reclaim our Royal Divinity, as we strengthen and balance our Ten Bodies and eight chakras, dump subconscious garbage, and clear past karma out of our auric field. With this spiritual science, we can actually rewrite our own destinies. I know it may sound very esoteric, but it can be extremely practical as well.

For example, when we fortify our Auric Fields (imagine a golden sphere around you), then we naturally have a protective force field around us, and negativity and illness cannot reach us. As we strengthen it further, we can hold wealth, conquer all obstacles, and attract good opportunities to us. As we clear and strengthen our Third Eye, we open up greater wisdom, intuition and discernment so that we can make better choices. As we activate our Throat Chakra, we are empowered to speak our Truth. As we heal our Heart Center, we are able to forgive ourselves and others, and give and receive love unconditionally. As we strengthen our Solar Plexus, we increase our willpower and ability to have good boundaries and manifest our will on earth. As we focus love on our Sacral Chakra, we can channel our passion, creativity and sexual energy in healthy ways. As we clear shame out of our Root Chakra, we can relax into belonging in this world.

And as we activate our Crown Chakra, we can embrace our primal Royal Divinity, and act as the Enlightened Leaders that we were born to be. I often tell people to envision a thousand petaled lotus on their Crowns, and cosmic lifeforce, golden mana, just pouring in, as we allow Spirit to bless us fully and be co-creators of our best lives.

All of this yoga, healing and self-development work is so that we may embody our full potential and be good stewards of all the gifts we are given in this short human life. And when we can prove to be able to hold and manage the blessings well, then the heavens can bless us with even more.

Yogi Bhajan once said, *"You are the highest of the incarnations. You are the crown of God's kingdom. Just wear the crown and keep your neck straight. Walk straight, walk tall. That's all it is. No left, no right. If you cannot keep your own crown on your head, you will live like a clown in your head. You decide."*

*   *   *

I believe that we live in a benevolent universe and that we have unseen ancestors and allies who are rooting for us, and for all of humanity. Spirit is waiting for us to step up and show up – *"soul on deck shines like gold in dark times"* as Clarissa Pinkola Estes exclaims. The more that we can handle, the more that we will be given. Spirit is ready to bless us and reward us for showing up and allowing our Highest Selves to take over. Good opportunities come to us all of the time, it is up to us heed the call, show up, and embrace it.

In my mind's eye, I imagine a vast expanse of infinite possibility, with an unfathomable number of potential timelines in a multidimensional grid, and some are lit up in gold and blaze through diagonally like "Magic Ziplines" – that if we can reach out with courage and faith, and grab hold and surrender, we can then ride a current of Spirit that transports us wondrously into a whole new reality and set of miraculous possibilities. If we allow it.

So make your mark. Take up space. Claim your Primal Divinity, this royal essence of who you truly are. Cultivate your character, integrity and dignity. Strengthen and fortify yourself so that you can be a Force of Goodness for your Self, your family, your community and the world. Conduct yourself like a Sovereign King/Queen, and rule over your domains with skill, wisdom, kindness and compassion.

Domains.
What do I mean by that, exactly?

A few decades ago, I took a course at Landmark called the Wisdom Course. It was a ten-month journey with five weekends all around the world, and I actually did it twice. One of my favorite exercises was when we created our Domains. Instead of being a victim and having life just thrown at you in a messy, reactive, random way; let's begin to consciously create our life by declaring what's important to us, delineating them and bringing them into the forefront of our lives.

So, bring to mind five to six areas of your life that are the most important to you, such as: Family, Partnership, Career, Health, Wealth, Spirituality, Home Space, Community, Creativity, etc. Write them on a piece of paper and draw a big circle around each one. Imagine them as spinning plates that you juggle and manage in your life. Or different garden beds that you are tending. These domains now make up your King/Queendom that you look after and cultivate.

Let's develop them further. Give each one a cool, inspiring name that makes you smile. Customize them by assigning them positive values and possibilities that you associate with each domain, so that they are meaningful to you. Write down a goal for each one that represents something concrete that you'd like to aim to accomplish in the next month / season / year. Check in regularly and feel into where you're at with the different domains, from a scale of one to ten, and start to manage and measure them, tend to and focus on them, as you take more control of your own life.

For example, here's a simple outline of my domains:

JADE'S DOMAINS:

1) Being One with Source
2) Nurturing Ohana (Family)
3) Supportive Partnership
4) Massive Abundance
5) The Radiant Lotus Way Programs
6) My Magical Lava Sanctuary

And a more fleshed out example of one of their possibilities and project so that you can envision this more fully:

The Radiant Lotus Way:

Possibilities: Fulfillment, Growth, Contribution, Magic, Joy, Abundance, Grace, Co-creating with Spirit, Soul Dharma ~

Projects:
1). Lead a sold-out Mastermind every Season
2) Have 2-3 Soul Clearings scheduled for every week
3). Earn $_____ every month as I support my family

(And there would also be Deadlines, Milestones, Resources, Structures of Fulfillment, etc, but that's another book for another time).

Along with embracing your Royalty and mastering your Domains, there are many other tools to help you master your outer reality.

For example, if you haven't yet, please write out a detailed outline of what you would like your Ideal Life to look like ten years out from now. Take some time to write down every detail of every aspect, such as – how old will you be, where will you live, who's around you, what kind of house do you live in, what kind of car do you drive, what have you accomplished already, what kind of quality of life do you enjoy, and how do you spend your time?

Write out your vision of your Ideal Life ten years out, and then turn a page, and reverse engineer it.

Write down, what does your life have to look like at five years out, to ensure that the ten-year vision is inevitable? (Example – if I have published four books already in my ten year, perhaps I have published two books by my five-year plan?). Now write it out with three years, then one year, then six months, then three months – all with the lens of what do I need to have accomplished and set in these time frames to make the ten-year vision a done deal, guaranteed and inevitable? You now have a guideline and some direction around what you need to do and focus on, to create your Ideal Life ten years out.

On every New Moon, I also do a simple ritual -- I think of three to five Dream Seeds that I'd like to see manifest in the next coming moon cycle, and I write them down. I then put that paper on my altar or post it on my mirror, and I also often share them in the group circles that I lead, as we all witness each other and add our love, prayers, support and encouragement for each others' dreams.

Besides keeping your Ideal Visions and Dream Seeds close to your heart and in your mind, I highly recommend instituting lots of sensory anchors to help keep you focused and call them into existence. For example, play mantras in the background all the time, burn incense or wear perfume that evokes your ideals, post up vision board type images onto your walls, fridges, mirrors, phones and laptop screensavers, etc. Write a check out from the universe for the amount of money that you'd like to call in. Listen to audio books and delta-theta meditations that program your conscious and subconscious mind towards what you want. That way, you are constantly surrounded by reminders that anchor you into what you are creating.

Consciously create your environment so that it is always calling you towards your highest self and ideal life. That way, even on days when you don't feel so great, your external environment will still call you into being your ideal possibility. Also, strive to live in a place that evokes your Soul nature. For me, living out here on the lava at the feet of one of the most active volcanos on earth, generally has me feeling pretty epic. All day and night, I'm communing with the elements and beautiful majestic nature. The sun beats strong on the ionic lava, and the wind and rain rush in to move stagnant energy quickly. It's hard to be upset here, when surrounded by so much glory. I am constantly inspired to be my Healer and Priestess Self out here, and people are constantly showing up at my door, asking for healing services. I never really needed to advertise.

So feel into what kind of living environment would suit you best, and perhaps do an astrocartology reading to find the most beneficial places on earth for you to visit, dwell, work at and thrive.

So, please, as you embrace your Royal Divinity, don't ever denigrate or desecrate yourself or others again. Be confident in who you are as a child of God and own your own beauty, wisdom, divinity and capacities. This doesn't mean having an ego complex, or feeling arrogant or superior to anyone else because all of us have this potential within us.

Life is short. Why not live it wildly, beautifully, majestically with wisdom, kindness, and compassion? If you can start to feel one with all of the nature around you and in this great web and woven tapestry of blessings that we all are in, you can begin to influence and create your own reality in a life-affirming way.

We all have so many innate gifts that just need to be awakened and cultivated. The Kundalini lifeforce sits dormant at the base of our spines until it is awakened to rise up through our chakras and revitalize all of our organs and every cell of our being. Some yogis who are very devoted and accomplished begin to develop "siddhis" – special powers and abilities. For example, it's said that Yogi Bhajan was able to command the rain and the water. Many of us are telepathic, clairvoyant, clairaudient, psychic, etc. So just know that so much is possible when we tap into and cultivate the treasures within us.

*   *   *

Last year was my ten-year anniversary for moving to the Big Island of Hawaii. After a decade of living here, through three different volcanic eruptions, through building multiple Temple spaces in jungles and lava fields, through homebirthing a handsome, half-wild little Tiger Bodhissatva boy, and through rising into my own power as a Sovereign Queen of my own domains, I felt I wanted to consecrate my Magical Lava Sanctuary again as the Adi Shakti Refuge for its next level of service. It would become a Creation Station for Artists and Visionaries to come and heal, create, write their book, launch their project, get

Soul Clearings to work through their blocks, and be pampered and empowered as they birthed their offerings.

I called upon my dear Hawaiian Kumu (teacher) – Kumu Hula Ali'I Kahuna Nui Ehulani Stephany -- to come on Spring Equinox and bless me and my Adi Shakti Refuge.

Kumu came dressed in red flowing robes and a gorgeous Haku Lei (crown of flowers). We faced the cardinal directions and blew the Pū (conch shell) at each turn, invoking the blessings of the spirits of all the directions including Father Sky and Mother Earth. She unfurled a hala mat in front of my Lava Temple and we chanted oli (traditional Hawaiian chants for wisdom, well-being and preservation). We gave offerings of awa (kava), olena (turmeric), awapuhi (ginger), alae salt (red clay salt), to the spirits that be. We took my offerings of the ti and noni leaf and tied it in a bundle and tied half to the ironwood tree near the Divine Mother Statue in front of the Temple and buried the other half at her feet. We walked the four corners of my property, sprinkling blessed water with a ti leaf along the way, consecrating this Refuge as a safe, sacred space.

And then Kumu turned to me and said, *"I have a gift for you, Jade."*

She brought out a second beautiful Haku Lei Crown and placed it on my head.

"Jade -- You are Mali'u. You are she who is well-salted and seasoned with Wisdom. She with depth of tone, deep sound and voice. A wisdom woman with a voice and sound that goes deep within one's healing work. Your gifts are a wonderful seasoning in one's life and in one's healing journey. Mali'u. This now is your Hawaiian name."

I bowed to her in deep thanks, we touched foreheads and shared three breaths.

*   *   *

Chapter 11:
When Heaven's Burning

*Someone I loved once gave me
a box full of darkness.*

*It took me years to understand
that this, too, was a gift.*

- Mary Oliver

Aloha Dear One, I thank you for your attention and your heart. I share all this with you in hopes of inspiring you to embark on your own healing journey to remove the rocks from your own Bowl of Light. So that you may enjoy and create the blessed life that you are meant to live.

I know it can get difficult. There's so much static and pressure from the world around us, and it can seem impossible to carve out any time, space or energy for yourself at all. As a single mother and sole provider for many years, I know what it's like to feel totally overwhelmed and desperate at times. And to have people tugging on you (physically and energetically), and only relating to you as a role that you play. And oftentimes, the people closest to you are not supportive, as they may be benefitting from you staying small and stuck where you are.

And I know that when we actually go on the journey, we will encounter all kinds of unforeseen obstacles and curveballs. There will always be challenges and problems.

Trust me, I know this well. I began writing this book in Spring 2018, but got interrupted when my beloved Kilauea Volcano began erupting.

Let me share with you some of the story...

Heaven's Burning

The earthquakes ramped up at the end of April 2018. First a few a day, then a few every hour -- and then every ten seconds. I had been housesitting a beautiful Temple Home in Leilani Neighborhood for the past season. Over a week, thousands of earthquakes were getting stronger and clearer and shaking the whole house. And then suddenly on May 3rd, Pu'u O'o crater on Kilauea volcano collapsed and all the lava drained out, now coming towards us --

"Lava is here! I repeat, lava is here!" Ikaika Marzo's voice came loud and clear through the Facebook live.

"This is no joke people, lava is erupting, I repeat – lava is erupting in Leilani Neighborhood right now! You must evacuate!"

"Holy!" I started mass-emptying drawers and throwing entire closets full of clothes into gaping suitcases. The gorgeous sunset blazed scarlet as the ground grumbled yet again.

"Mom, are we okay?" Eight-year-old Alaka'i gazed at me with big, brown, worried eyes.

"Yes honey, it's okay. Let Mom get our stuff, you can play with Legos for now."

For the next hour, I heaved suitcase after bulky suitcase in the slippery mud. The ground and the whole house was shaking every ten minutes --

"Alaka'i, we gotta go now!"

I grabbed my son and strapped him into my red, overflowing Honda Pilot and started backing out of the muddy, shaking driveway. Cracks were appearing in the road and power lines were falling down. I tightened my psychic warrior armor around my son and me and headed to my Lava Sanctuary twenty minutes away. I swore to the heavens, *"Dear Mother, help us through this."*

I left the red Honeymoon House in Leilani – Hawaiian for "Garland of the Heavens."

     *   *   *

The next day, Alaka'i and I woke up in sun-kissed Kalapana. We went on with business as usual. Dani, my caretaker at the time, started cleaning the Phoenix House and I sat on the Ohana House porch, checking the news when suddenly the 6.7 hit – the largest earthquake on the islands in four decades. We couldn't see straight as the whole house and lavafield violently shook for several minutes. Aftershocks continued for another seven months.

Over the next few months, the eruptions grew and grew, becoming the most destructive eruption in the timeline of Kilauea's volcano in more than two hundred years. It produced 320,000 Olympic-sized swimming pools' worth of lava that transformed the landscape and ultimately destroyed about seven-hundred homes.

The rushing lava also surrounded my ten-acre farm and rendered it inaccessible.

Back in 2012, I had bought a farm for my son's father to cultivate and live upon. I was happy on the sun-kissed lavafields of Kalapana, but William was an arborist and needed soil, trees and jungle. Although we were not together romantically, we were committed to be good co-parents to our child and to raise him with the best of our two worlds. So I bought the ten acres for William to live on and cultivate a food forest for Alaka'i to inherit someday. He called it "the Malama Ki Buddha Wisdom Garden," and it was meant to be a "pure land of elemental harmony."

We both toiled for years, me raising the money for it all, and William putting in the blood and sweat to develop it, as our son enjoyed the benefits of both parents and places. We ended up building three houses there, some meditation cabins, put in a thriving food forest, and even had a Stupa for Red Tara, commissioned and shipped from Indonesia. We had just finished building an outdoor kitchen and pouring in a concrete platform for the Stupa -- when the lava came.

Imagine a huge river of molten lava rushing at fifty-five miles-per-hour across your backyard and wiping out your neighborhood. The lava river took out Leilani, took out Pohoiki Road, took out our neighbors' homesteads, came super close -- and then paused at our gate -- and literally formed a diamond around the borders of my farm – and then took out everything else around it. Pele spared my farm, and the Red Tara Stupa, but made the farm unlivable and inaccessible. Trapped in a diamond of lava.

The lava continued to spread, swallowing up many of our most beloved natural spots. I cried when the beloved Ahalanui Warm Ponds got taken (a naturally occurring geothermal warm pond where I had celebrated so many of Alaka'i's birthdays growing up) and the Champagne Ponds where we had spent so many blissful afternoons. The lava kept going, vaporizing iconic Green Lake in minutes, and took out my son's Hawaiian Charter school, Kua O Kala, where he was attending first grade. A church in Hilo (an hour away) graciously allowed the school to continue there so the kids could finish out the school year. The lava river continued on, rushing to the ocean, forming thousands of miles of brand new land.

It became too toxic and dangerous to stay down in Kalapana.

The main Highway 130 -- and the only way in and out of Lower Puna -- started cracking and steaming in a dozen places. The skies blazed smoky blood all night and rained black strong sulfury soot during the day. We couldn't breathe well and I started having vertigo spells and falling to the floor.

Soon Mayor Harry Kim issued an evacuation of our district and for all tourists to leave. I had to close down my beloved Magical Lava Sanctuary at Pele's Feet, return six months' worth of reservations, and go into debt for the first time.

Community is a strong value here in Hawai'i, and many kind souls rose up to help many of us evacuees. Some friends -- Jay Jamal Boughanem and Kea Keolanui -- graciously opened up his Macnut farm just north of Hilo and transformed it into a little "lava refugee camp." So for six weeks, we camped with a few other evacuated families and an assortment of animals. I'd wake up, bring Alaka'i to school, drive an hour down to Puna, show proof of residency, don a gas mask, and try to secure my properties against looters. It was challenging because everything was off-grid and open-air. I had no locks on any doors. Actually, my Lava Temple didn't even have doors!

I boarded up the Temple and the other beloved tiny homes as best I could and installed a gate. The summer was an intense season full of heartbreak and purification; and a blur of evacuations, news of spreading lava, vertigo, toxic gases, lava raining green gems, and Pele's golden hair.

I played the "Sa Ta Na Ma" mantra on repeat – the one that I chanted when I did Kirtan Kriya for a thousand days when my son was born – it helped me keep calm during this crazy time. The seed syllables mean "Birth Death Infinity Rebirth" – integrating all the cycles of life.

I also stayed sane by tapping into Pema Chodron's wisdom frequency, with her audiobook -- *Things Fall Apart*. Her words washed over me while I drove all around Puna with a gas mask on trying to secure my properties. She assured me that life had always been uncertain, and to relax into the groundlessness of all existence. At night I would do the somatic exercises on myself, breathe deep and put my hands on my body, and ask myself the Quantum Questions –

"What's the good in all this? What's possible now that wasn't before? How is this actually blessing me?" I found that there was always still so much to be thankful for.

Lava finally stopped erupting ninety-two days later, in August.

In September, I was back in Kalapana and opened up my Sanctuary again. Puna had changed, a lot of my sweet community had left. It took a few months for life and tourism to get going again. And for me to get out of debt, but I persevered.

Thankfully, with the kindness of friends, life started getting back to normal.

After the dust had settled, my friend Jack Weber and I co-led one of the first Grief Circles for our community. He had lost his precious homestead in Kapoho that he had poured love on for eighteen years. It was a powerful, intimate experience hosted at my friend Fabi Vlchek's horse farm (another kind soul who was hosting a "lava refugee camp") and opened us up again to the ground of gratitude and community upon which we could stand no matter what was happening around us. It was such a gift to come together in safe, sacred space to shine light upon those aching tender places, together. Such a gift to witness and be witnessed, as we felt into the frozen feelings that we had pushed away before because well, lava was erupting, and we had to flee!

Such a gift to feel held and supported as we relaxed our "fight or flight" shocked nervous systems and began to pick up the pieces of our lives again.

With my farm surrounded and my beloved Lava Sanctuary closed down for six months, I found myself unexpectedly in debt, for the first time in my life. As the sole provider of my family, I knew I had to find another way to feed my family, that didn't depend on Hawaii tourism or the temperament of volcanos. I found that Spirit was pushing me out of my comfortable nest and having me fly. I needed to evolve my passions for teaching and healing into a full-fledged business and livelihood.

I prayed hard and Spirit said to me – "*Step up, show up, stop hiding! Write the book you've been wanting to write, be the Teacher you are meant to be, call in the Abundance that's there to be had. You are enough! And your son needs you…*"

And so I did. I created a series of workshops called *"The Gift in the Wound"* – helping people process grief and find the gift, the wisdom within the difficulty. I started teaching and coaching online, leading high-end Masterminds every season, on Sovereignty and Inner Mastery. I pulled myself out of debt and started investing in Business Mentors and Trainings to teach me the art of Sales, Marketing, Messaging, Launching, etc. – all the practical strategy and skillsets to balance out my strong mystical, intuitive nature. I was rebirthing myself newly and newly again. And learning how to hone and refine my gifts into building a solid, sacred business that could support my family and also help empower others. I learned to embrace Business as a Spiritual Path, as a University, as a Mantle and as a Crown. It was hard work, yet fun and fascinating as well.

Throughout my life, I've always had a natural instinct to build bridges, to harmonize and synthesize differences, to see the gifts and possibilities that are available in bringing together different worlds and modalities.

And now I was learning to marry the worlds of:

Money + Mana
Spirit + Strategy
Inner + Outer Mastery

To create ethical, blessed, soul-aligned Sacred Businesses.

I wanted to put Power & Money into the hands of the Dreamers, the Visionaries, the Artists, the Healers, the Mamas! I wanted to teach my SoulTribe the tools and skillsets to earn a good living, get their messages out there, and bless up their families and this world! I was passionate about teaching BUSINESS as an exciting, fulfilling, enriching Spiritual Path ~ and so I expanded my Radiant Lotus business to include offerings around integrating the fields of Money and Business as a sacred vessel of blessings as well.

*   *   *

So yes, dear one, life can often be unfair and full of pain. Unexpected tragedy can hit at any time. And it's up to us to learn to be the eye of the storm, our Sovereign Master, no matter what chaos might be happening around us, and to rest in the primordial ground of uncertainty. Life has always been uncertain and impermanent. That will never change. So when one can embrace this uncertainty as the ground of our being, we can move and flow and adjust as needed to the demands of the circumstances.

There are tons of tools that can help us to navigate these difficult times. And I've found that one of the most helpful and empowering keys to success in life is to have a supportive SoulTribe of trusted Allies to lean on. Life becomes so much more bearable, smooth, graceful, and fun when we consciously create a Council of Aligned Allies to share the journey with. And to have Wise Mentors who have already walked the road, to help guide us on our path. When we have a Mentor or have joined a Mastermind, this will save us a lot of mistakes and we will be able to jump timelines and embrace more opportunities. We don't have to exhaust ourselves reinventing the wheel. Instead, just team up with other conscious, like-minded Souls and observe and absorb wisdom from those who are already embodying what you would like to embody. And now that you are a Sovereign unto yourself, the greatest fun now is to collaborate within a community of other amazing Sovereigns and enjoy all the support that that offers.

* * *

Chapter 12:
Love Prevails All Trauma

"Love Prevails All Trauma."
– Harry Uhane Jim

We've covered a lot of ground here, and I'd like to recap the Phoenix Process that we just outlined.

We began by making a commitment to this path of Soul Work. We laid a foundation for the journey to unfold by setting intentions and carving out the time and space. We accepted our role as Master of it all and took responsibility for our whole life. We learned some ways to master our emotions and work through the triggers that come up. We explored the qualities of our mind and how to align with infinite wisdom. We dived into the power of conscious communication and how to use our word and our presence as our main manifestation tools. And we then embraced our royal divinity and shifted our focus outward to create the domains that make up our ideal life.

P: Pledge Allegiance to Your Soul & Its Purpose
(Make the Commitment & Set the Intentions)

H: Hold & Harness Your Sacred Time & Space
(Lay down the Foundation for the Journey to unfold)

O: Own Your Own Authority
(Being the Master & Exploring your Multidimensional Self)

E: Embrace Your Emotions, Honor These Messengers
(Mastering Emotions and Harnessing their Power)

N: Neutralize Your Mind, Align with Infinite Wisdom
(Transforming Limiting Beliefs into Empowering Ones)

I: Illuminate your Speech, Cultivating Conscious Communication
(Being Your Word, Generative Language, Silence & Presence)

X: Make Your Mark, Claim Your Crown and Master Your Domains
(Embody Your Royal Divinity & Create Your Ideal Life)

*   *   *

When I was seventeen, I had my first encounter with Unconditional Love from a fellow human being. I was a sophomore at Georgetown University. One night, I was extremely anxious and could not bear being alive. I had the bad idea of chugging a bottle of Jack Daniels and snorting some Xanax to try to relieve the weight of being conscious. I stumbled across campus and woke up my friend John at 1am.

I spent the whole night sitting in his dorm room, sobbing and spilling out all the unspeakable things that I had never told anyone, showcasing all of my shames, exposing all of the armor around my heart that I didn't even know had been constricting me for years. He just listened and cried. I went on for hours and he never interrupted me, just beamed compassion and cried with me. As the first rays of dawn arrived, my marathon flood of revealed shames dried up. I felt purged and emptied.

I looked at him humbly and asked, *"So, now that you know everything, everything bad that has ever happened to me, what do you think of me?"*

John looked intently at me for a long while. Then he answered slowly, *"Jade! I think you're the most beautiful thing in the entire world!*

My heart melted and cracked open. The shame suit shattered and shook off. A golden surge of relief, release and unspeakable joy beyond anything I had ever known before penetrated every cell of my Being. I spent the next day walking around raw and in awe, feeling empty and new. The whole world looked different. Cleaner and tinged with light. The sky encircled the world in a beneficent blue; even the sunlight felt like it was smiling at me. A world where I felt seen, safe and held for the first time in my adult life.

I had encountered the power of Unconditional Love and Divine Grace. The miracle that happens with someone holds space for others to dive deep and face their dragons, befriend their demons, air out all the secret skeletons pushed into the closet. The miracle of walking into the world again, reborn -- radiant like the Lotus -- pure and untouched, no matter what mud it grew up in. John had helped me clear my Bowl of Light. I knew that I would spend my life doing this for others as well.

This leaves me with these questions for you, Dear One:

Are you ready for this journey?

Are you ready to take the keys and unlock all those haunted houses?

Are you ready to welcome your Soul pieces back to yourself?

Are you ready to rise up like the Phoenix that you are,

Be the Master that you are, and take your rightful place as the Sovereign Divine Leader of your life?

I know that when you are ready, that Spirit will bless you completely. You will be empowered to live a glorious life beyond your dreams and fulfill your unique soul destiny. You will help others cross the rainbow bridges that you crossed, and your life will be a fountain of grace and blessings to others. You will become the Magical Temple in which God dwells.

I speak from experience.

My hand is here.

Reach out to me if you feel called.

With Infinite Unconditional Love Always,

Jade Rajbir Kaur (Queen of Courage)

Guerreira (Warrior Woman)

Mali'u (She who is seasoned with the sounds of wisdom)

       *   *   *

Acknowledgements

This book has been brewing within me for decades. In that meantime, I've edited twenty-six books for my father and several for others. I spent most of my life supporting other peoples' dreams. Then when my Hawaii Spirit Life happened, I felt like my life *became* a living poem, and it was just more important to *live it* in sheer conscious presence than to capture it in words.

After more than a decade here, I finally "graduated," and Spirit gave me a choice: I could either spend the winter editing a Ph.D. student's architecture thesis, or I could take the leap and write my own book. It's my habit to always choose the path of the most growth, so I threw my "hat over the fence" and decided to write my own book finally and use this as a lifeline into my next level.

And so, to The Author Incubator team: deep thanks again to Angela Lauria, CEO and founder for creating a brilliant program to help closet authors like me (who might never have published otherwise).

To my business partners at the Magical Lava Sanctuary: Will Beilharz, architect and creator of the Phoenix House; Sam and Erica Hawala, owners of the Ohana House; and Danny Lewin, my angel neighbor. Thank you for allowing the magic of Tutu Pele to give birth to your own creations on her sacred 'aina.

To all the amazing guests and retreatants who come and stay at this elemental vortex, thank you for hearing the call to come and spend some time communing with your own truest selves.

To my amazing assistants: Taryn Raine of The Remote Yogi, Lisa Disinger of JuicyVibes Media, thank you for all of your professional support, and my grounds team of Lava Angels -- thank you for making the Magical Lava Sanctuary shine day after day.

To my SoulTribe, all the angels who've shown up and supported me on this life journey, I am so thankful for your presence. Big Love to Jeff White, Eric and Zoey Faught, Darshan Mendoza, Kunana, William Collins, Evan Ragland, (and too many more to mention here) for your huge hearts and valuable support!

To the amazing Beings who heard the call and have joined my Radiant Queens / Soul Fire Sovereignty / Empress Pathway

Masterminds – thank you for your faith and trust and I am loving witnessing your blossoming into majesty!

To my first Soulmate who showed me Unconditional Love, John Donaldson. You saved me and inspired my whole life with your gift.

And to my beloved son, Alaka'i Ulimana Braham.
You are always the greatest treasure.

*   *   *

Thank You

Mahalo nui loa!

Deep thanks to you, Dear One.

I salute you on your journey, and I wish you the very best. I know it takes a great deal of Courage and Heart to embark upon the Radiant Lotus Way; and I'm so thankful for your commitment to your Soul and Ideal Life.

As a token of my gratitude, I've created a short video with a special meditation for you. Please visit my website to receive it.

And I would love to be part of your SoulTribe!

Please feel free to connect with me (I'm most active on Facebook and Instagram) and visit my site for more resources and other recommended resources.

I would love to empower you for a Season of Support in one of my programs, and/or welcome you to my Magical Lava Sanctuary in Hawai'i sometime soon!

I leave you with this traditional prayer that we usually end every Kundalini Yoga session with:

May the Long time Sun shine upon you
All love surround you
And the pure light within you
Guide your way on

Sat Nam!

~ PS ~

11/11/22
RESCUING THE RED TARA STUPA

Dear Friend,

After many years of healing from the intensity of losing access to my Farm and the Red Tara Stupa during the 2018 Eruption, I am finally ready to organize a "Rescue Mission" to gain access again and also liberate the Red Tara Stupa so that it may be of great blessing power to the people of Hawai'i and the world.

If you are interested in helping to support this project, please reach out to me.

Mahalo nui loa ~

JADE xoxo

Jade.truth@gmail.com

About the Author

Jade Chen (Rajbir Kaur) has worn many hats in this lifetime. Originally from New York City, Jade grew up in an artist family, immersed in her parents' humanist, multicultural views of a Global New Renaissance. She spent several decades assisting them in setting up Art Exhibitions, Cultural Events, Galleries, and Museums worldwide, in such notable venues as the United Nations, the State of the World Forum, UNESCO World Heritage Sites, five simultaneous museum shows during the Beijing Olympics, the World Expo, art fairs around the globe, as well as dozens of events and shows at their Cultural Center in SoHo NYC.

Having graduated Georgetown University (Dean's List, Lannan Fellow and summa cum laude), as well as earning her MFA in Creative Writing, Jade also writes, edits, and leads her own fusion of Yoga – Wellness - Writers' Retreats.

Throughout her intense life, Jade has immersed herself in mastering countless modalities of healing, wellness, and self-development work, primarily weaving Kundalini Yoga, Family Constellations, Martial Arts, Sat Nam Rasayan, and Soul Clearing.

She is a Certified Family Constellations Facilitiator, Kundalini Yoga Teacher, Tantric Love Coach, and Blackbelt in HapKiDo.

As the founder of The Radiant Lotus, Jade is a Spiritual and Business Mentor who empowers people to own their power, prosperity and magic fully. With the Divine Mother Frequency of Unconditional Love, Jade helps people to transform their trauma into treasure, re-access their infinite power, and uplevel all aspects of their lives. Some of her offerings include: Private 1:1 and Group Coaching, Soul Clearing Sessions, Ancestral Empowerment Ceremonies, as well as her seasonal Masterminds.

As the founder of the Adi Shakti Refuge, Jade hosts retreats for urban Souls to come "let the mud settle" and reconnect with their Primal Divinity.

Weaving the worlds of art, culture, wellness, yoga and healing spaces; Jade is also busy preparing to launch a Wellness Center at her family's new Art and Cultural Building in Midtown, New York City.

When she's not teaching in person there or online, Jade usually dwells at her Magical Lava Sanctuary, an off-grid, elemental refuge dedicated to the Divine Mother, located at the feet of an active Volcano on the Big Island of Hawaii.

Please contact if you'd like to work with her, visit her Lava Sanctuary, or help support our projects.

Mahalo nui loa! ☺

Website: www.theradiantlotus.org

Email: **jade@theradiantlotus.org**

Facebook: https://www.facebook.com/TheRadiantLotus1/

Instagram: @theradiantlotus

Made in the USA
Columbia, SC
18 February 2024

31495463R00102